ANSELM'S <u>PROSLOGION</u>: AN INTRODUCTION

R. A. Herrera

University Press
of America™

Library of Congress Catalog Card Number: 79-66421

PREFACE

One of the salient characteristics of contemporary medieval scholarship is the renewal of interest in Anselm's Proslogion argument. Few themes recur with such insistence. The argument and its later variations, phoenix like, always manages to rise from its ashes. Even Kant's 'definitive' refutation was rejected by Hegel, who credits Anselm with bringing the highest law to consciousness[1] while attempting a reformulation of the a priori demonstration, voiding the censure of the Transcendental Dialectic.

The Proslogion is one of the most important works of the Middle Ages, the center where a multiplicity of philosophical and theological themes converge, the point of departure for a veritable family of arguments for the existence of God. The text is still open to investigation due to the unhappy penchant of interpreters for arbitrarily reducing the argument to a few limited passages and excising it from its cultural ground. In this way, misinterpretations have been introduced into Proslogion interpretation and into the mainstream of ontological argument literature. The present task is a modest attempt to rescue the Proslogion from the ravages of time and the depredations of interpreters by viewing it within the context of Anselm's thought and culture.

In the past few decades alone, more has been written about the argument than perhaps any other comparable Medieval text. In a relatively unfriendly intellectual milieu, it has been given favorable treatment by Hartshorne[2], Malcolm[3], and Moreau[4], among others, while studies verging on the encyclopaedic such as Spicilegium Beccense[5], and Analecta Anselmiana[6], have, for the most part, centered on the argument. From the viewpoints of philosophy, theology, and religion, the influence of the Proslogion argument has been enormous, in spite of its paradoxically minor influence on Anselm's immediate disciples. It is possible, with Koyré, to classify Medieval and Modern philosophers as belonging to two major camps, those accepting the argument and those rejecting it. The argument stands at the very center of those problems which human thought has grappled with and been plagued by since Parmenides: the relation between thinking and being, actuality and possibility, God and man. To take a position here is to show one's hand on an entire constellation of philosophical and theological problems.

The contemporary approach to the Proslogion argument has, for the most part, followed later Medieval exegesis in consider-

iii

ing it primarily an exercise in dialectic, the logica vetus. Presently, new perspectives are being opened. Smith[8], Allshouse[9], and others have stressed the experiential factors found in the argument viewing Anselm as a philosopher-theologian of radical empiricism. Zubiri[10], and Dumery[11] believe that the argument can be interpreted in phenomenological or existentialist terms within the thematics of 'religacíon' and the 'fourth reduction'. The efforts of the present generation of exegetes is doubtless contributing towards a more comprehensive evaluation of the argument.

As previously noted, the Proslogion argument, in spite of the interest it elicits and the wealth of scholarship lavished on it, still remains, to a surprising extent, terra incognita. Many of its proponents and adversaries have remained curiously unaware of its original formulation. This may account for the uncritical manner in which most of our histories of philosophy assume the existence of an ectoplasmic 'ontological argument' which is, in turn, foisted on Anselm, Bonaventure, Descartes, Hegel and others. Even serious interpretation continues to center on Proslogion II in spite of Karl Barth's study (1913)[12] which demonstrated that the argument is far from being an isolated insight of the second chapter and that Proslogion II-IV, Gaunilo's defense, and Anselm's Reply must be taken into consideration.

It is surprising how little emphasis has been given to the unitary character of early Medieval thought. Philosophy, theology and religious experience were fused in a culture in which the Logos, second person of the Trinity, is root, source, and ultimate criterion of both religious life and reason. For Anselm, to be a believer, means to live both in God and in reason. The Proslogion argument can be understood only in the light of his cultural horizon, a commonplace which textual exegesis has all too often forgotten. Kemp-Smith has noted a characteristic of Medieval thought which is usually overlooked: that all the best medieval thinking is impassioned thought, charged with love and fear.[13] This is only a fairly safe generalization but goes to prove the point. Moreover, there is a widespread distaste and ignorance of the religious roots of Anselm's thought. Dom Jean Leclercq had done yeoman service in showing that from the eighth to the twelfth century it is possible to distinguish 'something like' two Middle Ages in the West, one monastic, the other scholastic.[14] The first is the continuation of Patristic culture in another age and civilization. The second is generated by the Carolingian renaissance, the town, the cathedral schools. Anselm scholarship tends to stress the scholastic while ignoring the monastic.

Viewed from the perspective of monastic culture the Proslogion argument presents itself as, what for want of a better term, can be called a gnosis. This was suggested by Gilson some four decades ago but was never fully developed either by him or

others.[15] By gnosis here is meant simply a praying in thought in
which the source of reality, truth, and justice, displays Himself
as existent. The Proslogion, in fact, takes the form of a pilgrimage within stability (peregrinatio in stabilitate) in which
the human soul endeavors to recover its original status, the
divine image becoming progressively more evident as it comes into
closer communion with the indwelling Trinity. Because of this,
Anselm cannot really be considered either as a rationalist or a
mystic, a dichotomy grounded on reason servered from religious
experience and peculiar to modernity. In the Proslogion reason
not only exercises the task of providing answers, constructing
demonstrations, but also engages in the therapeutic work of
purifying the mind, disposing it for an experience that transcends discursive reason.

It is difficult if not impossible to keep to the purely
scholastic (logical) interpretation once Proslogion XIV-XVIII is
given the attention which it merits. Although God has been found
cognitively He has yet to be experienced. Anselm makes it very
clear that this experience is the ultimate goal of the argument's
quest. His insistence does away with the naive misunderstanding
that the argument ends in Proslogion III or IV, the greater part
of the treatise being merely a pious afterthought. It is decidedly an integral part of the argument itself. Anselm, emulating
Plato and Augustine, simply shifts his attention from the product
of intellectual vision - the conclusion that God is greater than
can be thought - to the source of that light by which we 'see'
intellectually. The research for truth as known is expanded into
the search for truth as experienced.

A mystical interpretation of the Proslogion in the manner of
Dom Anselm Stolz must also be rejected. Anselm, in the argument,
arrives at a proof through necessary reasons, conclusions acceptable solely on rational grounds. The role of the Fool is to
bracket faith for the moment and allow reason to manifest itself
within its own domain. The description of God which is given
by faith - "that than which a greater cannot be thought" - must
be rationally justified. It is, in fact, 'unpacked' throughout
fifteen chapters of rather tortuous reasoning until the conclusion that God is greater than can be thought (Proslogion XV) is
attained.

Anselm, though not a modern rationalist may be considered
one within the context of Medieval Christianity. Reason cannot
generate faith but it does provide the seed of meaning out of
which faith may grow. Knowledge becomes the indispensable condition of faith: there is no faith without at least a minimal
degree of comprehension. Even the truths of faith revealed in
Scripture possess rational status although the human mind may not

be able to comprehend them in an exhaustive manner. The more one advances in understanding, the closer be approaches the vision of God.

As Anselm's notion of reason is an integral part of *Proslogion* interpretation it is necessary to refer to Anselm's other works. The relation between faith and reason cannot be understood without the *Epistola de Incarnatione Verbi* and the *De Concordia*. The much debated 'transition' between the real and conceptual orders, the cause of much dispute and confusion, cannot be understood without recourse to the *De Veritate*, and the relation between actuality and possibility can be adequately comprehended only in the light of *De Casu Diaboli*. Again Anselm's method will remain in obscurity if incursions into the *Cur Deus Homo* are neglected. Once *Proslogion* interpretation is extended beyond the usual limits our understanding will acquire additional depth. To do this it is necessary to first given a literal rendering of the *Proslogion* text and then proceed to deeper levels of analysis and interpretation.

The present study attempts to provide an introduction to the *Proslogion*, and make it comprehensible within the context of Anselm's work. The temptation to range farther afield and stop at further ports of call must be denied, as must any pretension of giving the last word on the *Proslogion*. It must rest satisfied to interpret the argument within the framework of Anselm's culture so as to continue the unearthing of its original meaning. Furthermore, it can hardly pretend to do more than introduce the voluminous 'ontological argument' literature and help to organize the field of *Proslogion* studies: to enter into minutiae would lie well beyond the archeological spirit of this investigation.

This interpretation of the *Proslogion* which includes an account of its historical vicissitudes should provide a point of departure for further incursions into Anselmiana and act as a bridge between the concerns of the serious student of Medieval Philosophy and those of the specialist. In attempting to remove some of the difficulties of *Proslogion* hermeneutic, Anselm's argument will be seen to possess a status unique in the history of philosophy, theology, and spirituality. These considerations bring us to the threshold of new, interesting, and complex inquiries and also to the end of the present introduction.

NOTES

1. G.W.F. Hegel, Lectures in the Philosophy of Religion (New
   York: The Humanities Press, 1962), III, p. 159 ff; Lectures
   on the History of Philosophy (New York: The Humanities Press,
   1965), p. 63 ff.

2. Charles Hartshorne, Anselm's Discovery: A Re-examination of
   the Ontological Proof for the Existence of God (LaSalle: Open
   Court, 1962).

3. Norman Malcolm, "Anselm's Ontological Arguments", in Philosophical Review, LXIX (1960), pp. 42-52.

4. Pour ou contre l'insensé (Paris: Vrin, 1967).

5. Spicilegium Beccense (Paris: Vrin, 1959). Edited by P.
   Grammont and the monks of the Abbaye Notre-Dame du bec.

6. Analecta Anselmiana: Untersuchungen uber Person und Werk
   Anselms von Canterbury (Frankfurt/Main: Minerva GMBH), five
   volume to date (1969-1976). Edited by K. Flasch, G. Geyer,
   H.K. Kohlenberger, C. Ottaviano, R. Roques, and R. W.
   Southern.

7. A. Koyré, Saint Anselme de Cantorbéry: Fides quaerens
   intellectum (Paris: Vrin, 1964).

8. John Smith, Experience and God (New York: Oxford University
   Press, 1968).

9. Merle Allshouse, An Evaluation of Anselm's Ontological
   Argument, (Unpublished Doctoral Dissertation) University
   Microfilms: Ann Arbor, No. 66-4877.

10. Xavier Zubiri, "Sobre el problema de la filosofía", in
    Revista de Occidente, Madrid, No. 118, Abril, 1933, p. 108ff.,
    also "Introduccion al problema de Dios" in Naturaleza,
    Historia, Dios (Madrid: Editora, Nacional, 1963).

11. Henri Duméry, The Problem of God in Philosophy of Religion
    (Chicago: Northwestern University Press, 1964).

12. Karl Barth, Fides quaerens intellectum: Anselms Beweis der
    Existenz Gottes im Zusammenhang seines Theologischen Programs
    (Zurich: Evangelischer Verlag, 1958).

13. "The Middle Ages, The Renaissance, and the Modern Mind",
    in The Credibility of Divine Existence: The Collected Papers
    of Norman Kemp-Smith (New York: St. Martin's Press, 1967),
    pp. 196-213.

14. Jean Leclercq, O.S.B., The Love of Learning and the Desire
    for God (New York: Mentor, 1962). See also Sofia Vanni-
    Rovighi, "Questo mirabilie secolo XII" in Studium, 54
    (1958).

15. He cited the gnosis of Clement of Alexandria to evoke the
    complexity and richness of the Proslogion. Etienne Gilson
    "Sens et nature de l'argument de S. Anselms" in Arch.
    d'hist. doct.et litt. du moyen age (1934), p. 49ff. Dom
    Jean Leclercq writes: "The Christian gnosis, the 'true
    gnosis', in its original, fundamental, and orthodox
    meaning, is that kind of higher knowledge which is the
    complement, the fruition of faith, and which reaches
    completion in prayer and contemplation...beyond a doubt,
    it is this comparison (to a gnosis) which gives the closest
    idea of St. Anselm's intellectual research, his applied
    dialectics, and mystical transcendence". Love of Learning,
    p. 215.

CONTENTS

CHAPTER I

THE AUGUSTINIAN BACKGROUND

Augustine's influence on Medieval thought is indisputable.
Christopher Dawson reflects this consensus when he states that
"the spirit of Augustine continued to live and bear fruit long
after Christian Africa had ceased to exist. It entered into the
tradition of the Western Church and moulded the thought of
Western Christendom so that our very civilization bears the
imprint of his genius."[1] Even an unsympathetic critic, Karl
Jaspers, credits Augustine with providing "the medieval con--
sciousness, amid an entirely different sociological and political
reality, with its foundations and spiritual weapons."[2] Anselm
and the _Proslogion_ argument live under the shadow of Augustine.

Anselm was an _Augustinus minor_ to his age, and though he did
reject some of Augustine's views, he cannot be comprehended in
isolation from this heritage. At least three works attributed to
Augustine include parts taken from Anselm: _De vita eremitica_ ad
diligendo Deo, and _De contritione cordis_.[3] The twelfth century
considered the _Monologion_ - a good argument can be made for considering the _Proslogion_ its continuation[4] - as another _De
Trinitate_.[5] Augustine was certainly Anselm's major authority and
besides him we can discern no larger influence than those of
Boethius and Lanfranc.

Anselm acknowledges his indebtedness to Augustine when he
attempts to justify the _Monologion_ to Lanfranc who was started
by the original character of the work. He has done no more than
rethink Augustine: "St. Augustine proved these points in the
great discussion in his _De Trinitate_, so that I, having as it
were uncovered them in my shorter chain of argument, say them on
his authority."[6] It is, in fact, the _De Trinitate_ which Anselm
cites most, and very likely his principal source.[7] However, in
Anselm's early works the name of Augustine is mentioned only once
and then probably the outcome of Lanfranc's displeasure. Southern, with some justification, speaks of the ambivalence of
Anselm's relations to Augustine.[8] Nevertheless, though the
education and circumstances of the two were dissimilar, one
formed by the cataclysmic upheavals accompanying the ruin of the
ancient world, the other by the monastic life and culture of the
eleventh century, a continuity of thought and theme is certainly
evident.

Anselm's age has been characterized as an 'age of innocence'
that in comparison to Augustine, Anselm suffered from a "certain

1

philosophical naivete."[9] This is an exaggeration although it is
true that Anselm's images and metaphors are the product of the
feudal and monastic world in which God and man are related as
Lord and vassal. Augustine's themes tend to become defleshed.
Even when Anselm goes off on an esoteric tangent when he deals
with the ratio of fallen angels to the elect, he falls short of
the abundance of Augustine dealing, say, with the properties of
numbers. Augustine is more than liberal in his quotations from
Scripture and always ready to substantiate his views by elaborate
exegesis. Anselm seems to do most of his serious reasoning outside of this domain[10] using scriptural quotations as a point of
departure for speculation and meditation. Some of the most
valuable elements of Augustine's thought are absent, notably the
historical insight of De Civitate Dei and the speculation on
rationes seminales.

    Anselm's account of the atonement rejects the rights of
Satan over mankind, a favorite Augustinian theme. He had too
uncompromising a view of God's dominion over creation to allow a
claim by a rebel: rebellion deserves only punishment. This
departure from Augustine led to difficulties regarding the Incarnation and his solution was accepted only by Abelard and his
disciples.[11] Again, the essential characteristic of freedom is
not freedom of choice but freedom from erroneous choice - restricted by Augustine to the elect - and nearly indistinguishable
from obedience. Further, if we are to credit the De Similitudinibus, Anselm could have at one time held the tripartite
division of the soul into reason, will, and appetite,[12] in place
of, or along with, the division into memory, reason, and will,
granting an independent status to appetite or desire.

    Anselm is not an Augustine written in small letters, dedi-
cated exclusively to transcribing the thought of the master.
Still, Augustine does provide the groundwork for the essential
themes from which the Proslogion is fashioned; God, the human
soul as vestigia trinitatis, knowledge and love, faith and reason.
The principle 'fides quaerens intellectum', and the description
of God as 'aliquid-quo-maius-nihil-cogitari-potest',can be traced
back to Augustine. A few remarks concerning Augustine and the
style of thinking that Anselm inherited may not be out of place.

                      Augustine and Paganism

    Whatever the extent of the influence of the ancient world,
especially Plotinus and the Stoics, on Augustine, we can agree
with Bréhier that "un Hellène avec ses traditions intellectuelles
ne pouvait ni admettre ni même comprendre les dogmes qu'intro-
duisait le christianisme: ni le monothéisme d'un dieu créateur,ni

                              2

la création elle-même, ni la chute, ni l'incarnation d'un sauveur, ni la notion même de salut comme transformation des choses."[13] Christianity, in the footsteps of Judaism, demythologizes the kosmos: divinity is restricted to the Trinitarian God and excludes soul, stars, the universe itself. Augustine believed the 'Platonists' were on the right track. They discovered that God was cause of the universe, light of truth, source of happiness. None the less, they ignored the only medium of access to their goal - Christ - because they lacked humility.[14] While Greek philosophy is astounded primarily by the changeableness of things within the kosmos, viz. in its sublunary part, Augustine is astounded by its intrinsic non-being. While the classical mind philosophizes from the perspective of being, the medieval and modern mind philosophizes from the perspective of nothingness.[15] Creation is an outrage to the classical mind as it violates the unity of reality and negates the eternal, necessary, and hierarchically ordered procession.[16] But from Augustine's vantage point, if the truth will make you free, it frees you above all from the kosmos, the mundus.

Augustine seems to think that the Greek view of man is deficient, because it viewed man as merely a thing among other things. It has its origin in knowledge about things, in nature. On the contrary, the way to the knowledge of man is through man himself, through interiority. This journey into the self, the early Medieval peregrinatio in stabilitate, is both a withdrawal from the mundus but also an entry into the truth which is above: "Noli foras ire in te ipsum redi, in interiori homine habitat veritas: et si tuam naturam mutabilem inveneris transcende et te ipsum."[17] Reason does not enter into itself because it already knows itself, but by entering into itself it is able to know itself.

The Christian detaches himself from nature for the sake of truth. As God is eternal truth, to live in truth is both to live in God and in reason. Philosophy is transfigured into a 'holy doctrine', the light of the gift of wisdom making use of reason,[18] which encompasses the whole domain of theology, philosophy, and practical moral science. Reason, illuminated by faith, is now directed through love to the fruition of God: "verus philosophus amator Dei."[19] Greek theoria is transformed into Christian contemplatio.

Principal Notions

Love (amor) has especial importance as it measures the permanence of revealed truth[20] and creates a unity between the human soul and God, binding them together as lover and beloved.[21] Heir

to the Platonic _eros_, love acts as a gravitational principle pro-
pelling the soul towards its object: _pondus meum_, _amor meus_. All
men who love truth for its own sake are joined in a special way
and directed towards that Truth which is the source of all
truth.[22] In this way, the soul begins to take the shape of truth
(_incipit configurari veritati_) ascending towards God.[23] Augustine will not hesitate to describe our knowledge of God as God's
existence in us, and the growth of that knowledge as the growth
of God in us.[24]

The very first sentence of the _De Trinitate_ faults those men
who are led astray by immature and perverse love of reason, and
launches an attack against those who hold erroneous opinions
about God.[25] The mind must be purified "to ineffably contemplate
the ineffable". Faith effects this purification.[26] As God is
within man to search for God in the outer world may well bring
about a loss of innerness which is the privileged medium of
access to God: "_Ecce Deus dilectio est: utquid imus et currimus
in sublima caelorum et ima terrarum,quaerentes eum qui est apud
nos, si nos velimus esse apud eum._"[27] To know God and to adhere
to Him is the privilege of the clean of heart, and faith is the
means by which the heart is purified and disposed for knowledge
in this life and vision in the next.[28] The human mind as the
privileged point of departure for the demonstration of God's
existence and the need of living faith as the agent of cognitive
purification are taken whole cloth into the _Proslogion_.

Augustine, as later Anselm, insists that to think about God
as God should be thought of is not solely a cognitive under-
taking. The will must add its command; truth must be sought
piously, diligently, and chastely.[29] Only a proper disposition
overcomes the residue of sin and pride of spirit which bars the
way to truth. Not limited to the cognitive realm, truth trans-
forms and structures the soul. The work of doing what is right
precedes the delight of knowing what is true.[30] Sin and insuf-
ficient moral purification are effective obstacles to the knowledge of God. Augustine speaks of this state as a sort of insani-
ty.[31] The Fall is the root of the corrosion which pervades human
nature and it can be corrected only by God. Through grace man is
made holy and the freedom of Adam (_posse non peccare_) gives place
to the possibility of having the ultimate freedom of the saved
(_non posse peccare_).

No one can be completely ignorant of God: "no one can know
Him as He is, but no one is permitted not to know Him." [32] Perhaps because of this belief he elaborates proofs through universal consensus [33] and order in the universe,[34] in addition to his
favorite demonstration based on eternal and unchangeable truth.[35]
Portalié cites texts to the effect that all proofs show that God
does, in effect, exist, but not that He ought to exist.[36] This

would seem to rule out the Proslogion demonstration, but the
very fact that Anselm, in the Monologion, essays a proof similar
to Augustine's, returning to it in the later De Veritate, shows
that he was open to Augustine's approach. Augustine's emphasis
on God's simplicity aptly reflected in his choice of essentia
over substantia[37] and on God's eternity transcending space and
time,[38] probably influenced Anselm's argument. For Augustine,
the being of God is the highest and most complete form of being
and is unchangeable.[39] Vignaux indicates that the originality
of the Proslogion consists in the conversion of Augustinian
notion of absolute divine grandeur into a dialectical principle,
de se per seipsum probat, synthesis of "pure mechanism" and
"animated thought".[40]

Belief precedes understanding: "we believe that we may know,
we do not know what we may believe."[41] Augustine, as later
Anselm, postulates a type of knowledge prior to the understanding
of revealed truth. Although faith precedes reason regarding
"deeper truths", reason precedes faith in concluding that faith
is itself reasonable.[42] Augustine invokes the authority of
Isaiah 7:9 ("unless you believe, you shall not understand,"):
"although no one can believe in God unless he understands something, he is nevertheless enabled to understand more by the very
faith which he believes. For there are some things which we do
not believe unless we understand and some others which we do not
understand unless we believe."[43] Anselm will add precision and
clarity to this distinction.

Bréhier observes that Augustine was attacking Hellenic rationalism in his polemic against Pelagius who seemed to rule out
prayer and the life of spirituality.[44] The close relation
between faith and reason which is found in the Contra Academicos
is a constant in Augustine's later works: wisdom is directed
toward union with God. This conception of the eminently religious character of knowledge finds a champion in Anselm. Augustine teaches that the soul can be so glutted with material images
that it loses itself and can find itself only by penetrating that
layer of sensations which constitutes a nearly impenetrable
crust.[45] Faith directs the human soul inwards (to his true self)
and upwards (where God teaches and can be remembered), to that
state in which the soul is docile to God's continuous presence.[46]
If, as Gilson indicates, memory of God is only an example of
God's omnipresence,[47] then we may have here a further adumbration
of the Proslogion argument.

In the De Trinitate, Augustine advises the reader to
increase the light of the sun as far as his imagination is able,
then multiply it innumerable times. Even this would not be God.
If all the angels were comprised into one being and their number
milia milium, this entity would still not be God. God is light,

that light which the heart recognizes when it hears 'Veritas est!', before the weight of sinful nature dissipates the force and initial clarity of this insight.[48] God is the sun of the soul, the inner Teacher, the light, (the soul is the eye),[49] the 'pater intelligibilis lucis' and pater illuminationis nostrae',[50] the principle of intelligibility and the cause of knowledge, and a being a greater than which cannot be thought.[51]

The human soul is created in the image and likeness of God, and in De Trinitate VIII, Augustine examines the vestigia trinitatis. The Trinity of lover, beloved, and the love which unites them is reflected on the human level by the mind (mens), knowleedge (notitia) and love (amor), each member coequal yet possesing its own distinct identity.[52] The Trinity of memory (memoria), understanding (intelligentia), and will (voluntas), is given and further developed in De Trinitate XIV. The mind is habitually remembering, understanding, and loving itself, emulating the Trinity.[53] But this imitation is faulty and requires a turning of the soul (conversio) to God by faith to perfect and strengthen it: to be an image of God is to remember, understand, and love Him, "quod cum facit, sapiens ipsa fit".[54]

Man possesses one basic reason (ratio) which can turn either towards sensible things (ratio inferior) or immutable truth (ratio superior). The first constitutes knowledge (scientia), the second wisdom (sapientia).[55] Knowledge is hierarchically ordered towards its completion in wisdom, itself directed towards ultimate vision.[56] This conception will be kept more or less intact throughout medieval Augustinianism and is faithfully reflected in the Proslogion.

The highest truths are seen, by the human mind, "in quadam luce sui generis incorporea",[57] a sort of incorporeal light of its own kind. Both knowledge and wisdom require this noetic principle. Illumination is a particularly vexatious problem for Augustinian scholarship as it is related to the question of Augustine's neo-platonism. In point of fact Augustine seems to have considered Plotinus' theory of illumination as consonans Evangelio and grounded on the Gospel of St. John.[58]

God is the Teacher, the inner master, the source of agreement between minds: "in una schola communem magistrum in caelis habemus.[59] As previously stated He is the 'sun' and the soul the 'eye'. We contemplate truth by means of an incorporeal light analogous to the manner by which the bodily eye sees in corporeal light, "menti hoc est intelligere, quod sensui videre."[60] As the sun is the source of that light which makes all things visible, God is the source of that light which makes all truth visible.[61] If man is wise through participation in God's wisdom is this participation natural, supernatural or both? An interesting

6

text of _De Trinitate_[62] would incline to the latter solution although as Gilson points out, "the insistent repetition of the
terms _natura_ and _naturalis ordo_, as well as the affirmation that
this nature and natural order were created by God prove beyond
doubt that the whole cognitive process moves within the limits
of nature." [63]

Though Gilson's opinion may be debated[64] there is no doubt
that the 'divine light' shines for all men and thought takes
place only in its light. The aspect of knowledge which most
impressed Augustine was the sovereign independence of truth, it's
authority over individual minds. The human mind remembers the
'_regulae iustitiae_' as they are inscribed "_in libro lucis illius
quae veritas dicitur_", passing from Truth to man "_sicut imago ex
annulo et in ceram transit, et annulum non relinquit_",[65] as the
image passes from the ring into the wax without leaving the ring.
The image is used several times by Augustine.[66]

Portalié is on weak ground indicating that illumination
produces "the impressed species which the Aristotelians attribute
to the agent intellect."[67] On the contrary, illumination takes
the human intellect for granted,[68] and would be rather grotesque
in the role of a cognitive prosthesis. Boyer[69] and Gilson seem
to be more to the point in affirming that the intellect sees the
truth of its judgments, not the content of ideas, in the light
of illumination.[70] As Gilson states, paraphrasing Augustine,
"experience and not illumination tells us what an arch or a man
is, illumination and not experience tells us what the perfect
arch or perfect man ought to be."[71] On a higher level, this
light, _supra mentem_, the root of knowledge, becomes the goal of
spiritual life. Augustine borrowed his terminology from Neo-
platonism and the imagery of the _phos hen photos_ is better suited
to depict atemporal and eternal generation from the One than the
doctrine of creation.[72] Yet, Augustine's theory of illumination
became an important part of the philosophical, theological and
mystical heritage of the Middle Ages. It was accepted by
Anselm, though not without modification.

Summary

Our preceding observations indicate that Anselm is heir to
Augustine's theological and philosophical presuppositions, his
faith and spirituality. He inherits a universe of discourse
covering the entire drama of God, creation, the fall, and salvation, in particular the _Proslogion's_ description of God,[73] the
credo ut intelligam,[74] even the Fool's denial of God's existence.[75] He follows Augustine in believing that wisdom arises
from faith, that faith is the corrective and purifying agent of

the mind, that the mind in its functions of memory, understanding and will is the image of the Trinity and the privileged point of departure for any ascent to God. Wisdom is ultimately an _itinerarium mentis in Deum_ and reasoning a praying in thought directed toward ultimate vision. Anselm's 'method' in the _Proslogion_ is basically Augustinian innerness issuing into a quest for transcendent truth powered by love. Finally, in this far from exhaustive summary, the notion of God as Supreme Truth is found in many of Anselm's works and becomes the point of departure for his notion of rectitude.

Anselm is also indebted, although to a far lesser degree, to other sources--Aristotle as transmitted by Boethius is not absent--and his Augustinianism is definitely of a monastic cast. Aside from the few departures from Augustine, we find in Anselm original insights such his notions of rectitude, freedom, and the interconnection between faith and reason which led to the accusation of 'immoderate philosophism' by more than one critic.[76] At present, conscious of the paramount importance of Augustine's influence, that "son point de départ est tout augustinien",[77] let us turn to the _Proslogion_.

NOTES

1. Christopher Dawson, "St. Augustine and His Age", in A
   Monument To St. Augustine (London: Sheed & Ward, 1930),
   pp. 38-39.

2. Die Grossen Philosophen I (München: R. Piper & Co., Verlag,
   1957), trans. by R. Manheim, Plato and Augustine, ed. H.
   Arendt (New York: Harcourt, Brace & World, Inc., 1962),
   p. 115.

3. Eugene Portalié, "Saint Augustine", in Dictionnaire de
   Théologie Catholique, trans. R.J. Bastion, A Guide to the
   Thought of Saint Augustine (Chicago: Henry Regnery, 1960),
   pp. 74-75; 352-353.

4. The Monologion proofs have their point of departure in the
   contingent and relative and need supplementing by a proof
   based on the necessary and absolute. The Proslogion is, in
   this view, intended to be read as the extension of, or
   appendix to, the Monologion. In fact the Monologion proofs
   are actually presupposed. Nineteenth century historians
   tended to base the Proslogion II augument on the Monologion
   proofs: Bouchitte,de Remusat, Stokl, Van Weddingen. Refer
   to Arthur C. McGill "Recent Discussions of Anselm's Argument",
   in The Many-faced Argument, p. 103, Note No. 225.

5. Note the similarity between the Monologion proofs for the
   existence of God and De Trinitate, VIII, 3.

6. Ep. 77 (Opera III) 199, 17-26.

7. He cites Augustine directly only six times, four times from
   the De Trinitate. See Anselm, Opera Omnia, Vol. VI, p. 21.

8. R.W. Southern, St. Anselm and His Biographer (Cambridge:
   C.U.P., 1963), pp. 31-32.

9. Ibid., p. 352.

10. John McIntyre, St. Anselm and His Critics (Edinburgh: Oliver
    and Boyd, 1954), p. 48ff.

11. Southern, op.cit., p. 96. In substituting the notion of a
    conflict between God's grace and the rights of Satan with
    the synthesis of God's goodness and justice as raison d'être

for the Incarnation, Anselm may seem to deprive the act of atonement of its concrete, historical, status.

12. De Sim., CLXX. The Liber de Similitudinibus is a large collection of sayings attributed to Anselm. Twelfth century manuscripts are scarce but begin to be common in the Thirteenth and by the Fourteenth is usually included among Anselm's works. See Southern, op. cit., pp. 221-226.

13. Émile Bréhier, "Logos Stoïcien, Verbe Chrétien, Raison Cartésienne" in Études de Philosophie Antique (Paris: P.U.F., 1955), p. 166.

14. Confessions, VII, 9. De Civitate Dei, X, 29.

15. Among others, refer to Xavier Zubiri's little known "Sobre el problema de la filosofía", in Revista de Occidente, No. 118 (April, 1933), p. 91.

16. Bréhier, op. cit., p. 168ff.

17. De Vera Religione, XXXIX, 72.

18. This is the contention of Jacques Maritain, "Thomism and Augustinianism", in The Degrees of Knowledge (New York: Charles Scribner's Sons, 1959), p. 294.

19. De Civitate Dei, VIII, 1

20. De Moribus, I, 17, 31.

21. De Trinitate, VIII, 10, 14.

22. De Ordine, II, 18, 48; Confessions, XII, 25, 34.

23. De Ordine, II, 19.

24. "Crescat ergo Deus, qui semper perfectus est, crescat in te; quanto enim magis intelligis Deum et quanto magis capis, videtur in te crescere Deus". In Joh. Ev., III, 16.

25. De Trinitate, I, 1, 1.

26. Ibid., I, 3.

27. Idem.

28. Ibid., VIII, 4, 6.

29. See De Quantitate Animae 14, 24; De Vera Religione 10, 20;

De Moribus Ecclesiae I, 1, 1; De Ordine II, 19, 61; Epistola 140, 19, 48.

30. Contra Faustum XII, Soliloquia I, 1, 3.

31. Enarrationes in Psalmos, 13, 2; 52, 2; Sermo 69, 2, 3.

32. Enarrationes in Psalmos, 74, 9.

33. In Joannis Evangelium Tractatus CXXIV, 106, 4.

34. Sermo 141, 2, 2; Confessiones X, 6, 9.

35. De Diversis Questionibus LXXXIII, 54; Confessiones VII, 10, 16. It is worked out in detail in De Libero Arbitrio II, 3, 7; II, 15, 39. Beginning with that which is most excellent in man, reason (ratio), he concludes to the existence of something superior to it, unchangeable truth: "ac per hoc eam manifestum est mentibus nostris, quae ab ipsa una fiunt singulae sapientes, et non de ipsa, sed per ipsam de caeteris indices, sine dubitatione esse potiorem". (II, 14, 38). If there is something more excellent than truth, then this is God, if not the Truth is God: "Si enim aliquid est excellentius, ille potius Deus est: si autem non est, nam ipsa veritas Deus est." (II, 15, 39). God, then, does exist, "Est enim Deus, et vere summeque est." (Id.). It should be noted that Augustine's argument leads to the second person of the Trinity, Wisdom engendered and equal to the Eternal Father Id.).

36. Epistola 142, 2; of. Epis. 160, 1-3.

37. Substantia introduces a distinction between the essence of a being and its accidental qualities. See De Trinitate VII, 5, 10,

38. De Genesi ad litteram libri XII, V, 5, 12; Epistola 137, 28.

39. De Civitate Dei, XII, 2ff.

40. Paul Vignaux, Philosophie au moyen age, trans. by E.C. Hall, Philosophy In The Middle Ages (Cleveland: Meridian, 1959), P. 43. Refer also to pp. 37-41.

41. In Joannis Evangelium Tractatus CXXIV 40, 89; De Trinitate, VIII, 5, 8; IX, 1, 1.

42. Epistola 120, 3.

43. Sermo, 43, 7, 9; Enarrationes in Psalmos 118, 18, 3.

44. Emile Bréhier, Histoire de la philosophie: L'Antiquité et le Moyen Age II: Période Hellénistique et Romaine (Paris P.U.F. 1931), trans W. Baskin, The Hellenistic and Roman Age (Chicago: University of Chicago Press, 1965), p. 244.

45. De Trinitate X, 5, 7; X, 8, 11; X, 9, 12.

46. Ibid., XIV, 15,21ff.

47. Étienne Gilson, The Christian Philosophy of Saint Augustine (New York: Random House, 1960), p. 104.

48. De Trinitate VIII, 2, 3.

49. De Genesi ad litteram libri XII, 31, 59; De Peccatorum meritis I, 25, 38.

50. Soliloquia I, 1, 2; De Moribus Ecclesiae I, 17, 32; For Plotinus see De Civitate Dei X, 2. Gilson points out that the Scriptural texts come from John I, 6-9; 16, the basis for the comparison between God and the sun. Op. cit., p. 288, note 36.

51. Confessiones, VII, 4, 6.

52. De Trinitate, IX, 4, 4. Ibid., IX, 8, 13.

53. Ibid., XIV, 8, 11.

54. Ibid., XIV, 12, 15.

55. Ibid., XII, 3, 3. See also J. Rohmer, "Sur la doctrine franciscaine des deux faces de l'homme", in Arch. d'histoire doct. et lit. du moyen age II (1928), pp. 73-77.

56. Bourke calls it "a method of intellectual contemplation which finds its climax in the celestial vision of the eternal, incorporeal, and immutable things of God". Vernon J. Bourke, Augustine's Quest of Wisdom (Milwaukee: Bruce, 1944), p. 221.

57. De Trinitate XII, 15, 25; XII, 13, 25; XII, 14, 22.

58. Confessions VII, 9, 13. Refer to Note #50.

59. Sermo 298, 5, 5; Cf. Sermo 23, 2, 2. Also note Gilson's remarks in op. cit., p. 74ff.

60. De Ordine II, 3, 10; Soliloquia I, 6, 12; De Trinitate XII, 15, 24.

61. Soliloquia I, 6, 12.

62. De Trinitate, XIV, 12, 16.

63. Gilson, op. cit., p. 79.

64. The boundaries between the natural and the supernatural in the cognitive process is tenuous and it seems rather hazardous to plot out clear cut domains.

65. De Trinitate, XIV, 15, 21.

66. Enarrationes in Psalmos 4, 8, and De Ordine II, 8, 25.

67. Portalié, op. cit., p. 113.

68. See Gilson, op. cit., p. 79.

69. Charles Boyer, L'Idee de la Verite dans la Philosophie de Saint Augustine (Paris: Gabriel Beauchesne, 1922), p. 206ff., and also Christianisme et Neo-Platonisme dans la Formation de Saint Augustine (Paris: Gabriel Beauchesne, 1920), p. 189ff.

70. De Trinitate IX, 7, 12. See Boyer, L'Idee de la Verite, p. 212; Gilson, op. cit., p. 86ff; Portalie, op. cit., p. 113ff.

71. Gilson, op. cit., p. 90.

72. E. Bréhier, "Logos", p. 168ff. Also "Mysticisme et Doctrine chez Plotin", in Études, pp. 225-231.

73. Confessions I, 7, 4; De Doctrina Christiana, I, 1, 7.

74. In Joannis Evangelium Tractatus CXXIV, XL, 9; Sermo CCXII, 1; Sermo LXXXIX, 4; De Trinitate I, 8, 5.

75. Enarrationes in Psalmos, LII, 2.

76. See especially Josef Pieper, Scholastik trans. R. Cercos, Filosofía Medieval y Mundo Moderno (Madrid: Ediciones Rialp, 1973), pp. 67-93. He maintains that Anselm was the Medieval Christian philosopher least affected by the 'spirit' of the Pseudo-Denis and this led to an over-valuation of ratio, a ratio which does not capitulate before mystery but only before a clearer, more powerful, argument. Also E. Gilson, History of Christian Philosophy in the Middle Ages (New York: Random House, 1955), p. 129.

77. P. Rousseau, Oeuvres Philosophiques de Saint Anselme (Paris: Aubier, 1945), p. 48.

CHAPTER II

THE PROSLOGION ARGUMENT

Anselm, as well as his biographer, Eadmer, stress the unique
character of the _Proslogion_ argument. Although the possible formulation of such an argument fascinated him, Anselm states that
it repeatedly evaded him, and so he decided to discard it.[1]
Eadmer, something of a hagiographer, insists that the tenacity
and persistence with which the formulation of the argument im-
portuned him, was taken by Anselm to be a diabolical temptation
endangering his peace of mind and fidelity to monastic observ-
ance.[2] While suffering from this intense inner conflict the
definitive formulation came to him and was eagerly and joyfully
received.[3] Perhaps to emphasize the miraculous nature of this
discovery Eadmer narrates a rather curious story. The original
formulation of the argument, written on tablets, was lost and a
second redaction destroyed. Anselm finally had the argument
transcribed on parchment and in doing so expanded the original
argument into a 'small book'.[4] The _Proslogion_, as it is found
in Schmitt's critical edition, covers twenty-nine pages.

The preface outlines the goals of the _Proslogion_ which will
be developed in its twenty-six chapters. Anselm proposes to give
a unique, self-grounding argument "one single argument that for
its proof requires nothing besides itself".[5] It is advisable to
understand 'argument' in a wide sense, one not restricted to,
though including, strict rational proof.[6] This single argument
sets out to demonstrate that (1) God really exists; (2) He is
the Supreme Good grounding all things; and, (3) whatever else
Christians believe about the Divine Substance: "et quaecumque
de divina credimus substantia".[7] Let us review these points.

The first two present little difficulty. Anselm has taken
it upon himself to provide a proof for the existence of God, and
to uncover certain implications related to His Supreme Goodness.
But what of the third: whatever else we of the Christian faith
believe about the Divine Substance? This will not directly apply
to all the particulars of the Christian faith but, as can be
evidenced by the _Proslogion_ text and the Reply, will be represented by a nodal principle, out of which the particulars may be
deduced.[8]

The _Proslogion_ is written "from the point of view of one
trying to raise his mind to contemplate God and seeking to under-

stand what he believes".[9] Here we encounter a typical Anselmian
fusion of the spiritual and the intellectual: two goals are
posited, the understanding of what is believed and the contemplation of God. Knowing and spirituality become two aspects of
the ascent to God. In this raising of the mind, Anselm establishes a correlation between knowledge, self-perfection, knowledge of God, and approximation to ultimate vision. Understanding
and contemplation are aspects of one aspiration.

But does not mean that the _Proslogion_ is restricted to the
monk, even to the believer. It is a monk and a believer who
discovers and presents the argument, but, as Anselm states in the
Epistola de Incarnatione Verbi, his purpose was to show that it
is possible to prove by necessary reasons, apart from Scriptural
authority, those things held by faith concerning the divine nature, with the exception of the Incarnation.[10] The argument is
open to all, the Fool included as an allocution in which faith
goes in quest of understanding (_fides quaerens intellectum_), a
rousing of the mind to the contemplation of God.

Chapter I: Theological Presuppositions

The first chapter provides the theological reservoir of the
Proslogion, the ground of its later development, the context in
which the dialectical sections that follow are to be placed.
Anselm begins by addressing himself (and others) as _homuncio_,
insignificant man, a term which he often uses to describe fallen
humanity.[11] This chapter discusses the characteristics of this
condition and the possibility of returning to man's original,
uncorrupted, state. It is heavily tinged with emotion and we
can note why Anselm is credited with having introduced into a
tradition still Carolingian in temper, a new style of personal
passion and emotional extravagance.[12] Man is in exile, in blind-
ness as the _patria_, the _visio dei_, have been lost. Still seeking
goodness, peace, and joy, fallen man encounters confusion, tribu-
lation, and anguish.

God's image is present in man, no matter how darkened and
effaced it may be: "You have created Your image in me, so that
I may remember you, think of You, love You".[13] If God is everywhere, and present in a special manner in man, why then is His
existence not manifest? Why is God not present? The human soul,
created in God's image, does not experience God, it does not do
that which it was created to do: "I was made in order to see You,
and have not yet accomplished what I was made for".[14] This al-
ienation of the soul from its proper function caused by original
sin displaces God from the center of man's concern. He no longer
faces God but is, to use a favorite expression of Anselm's

16

"curved" so as to face himself.

Man can do nothing to rectify this condition: "this image is so effaced and worn away by vice, so darkened by the smoke of sin, that it cannot do what it was made to do unless You renew and reform it".[15] This section is full of Scriptural texts of petition: for God to 'hear', 'be mindful', 'help', and so forth. They are presented one after another to the point of excess, stressing the Divine initiative that is the ground for the renewing of God's image in man as well as for the exercise of reason that follows: "I can neither seek You if You do not teach me how, nor find You unless You reveal Yourself".[16] The only 'method' that can be used is to concentrate on God, casting aside all cares and preoccupations. "Intra in cubiculum mentis tuae", Anselm advises, shut out all thoughts except those of God and those that can aid in this quest.[17] The resemblance to Descartes' procedure at the very beginning of the third meditation is obvious[18] and will be discussed later. In this way Anselm proposes to effect a reduction of all that is not God nor oriented towards Him. Only in a space in which the world's clamor is absent can the heart speak to its Lord. This is obviously a variation if not a repetition of a basic Augustinian theme.

Anselm, following scriptural tradition, views the heart as the root and source of inner truth: to say in one's heart is equivalent to thinking (cogitare). Something can be "said in one's heart" or thought in two different ways as Proslogion IV indicates: when the word signifying it is thought, and when the thing itself is understood.[19] The transition from the first to the second, from vox to res, the core of Proslogion II-III, presents interesting possibilities for investigation.

This first chapter is then a theological and spiritual prolegomenon to the argument. It emphasizes the quest for the renewal of the trinitarian image in man, and the need for God's aid to assure its success. Faith is viewed as the point of departure for understanding, that partial understanding of God's truth which is adequate to the human mind: "nisi credidero, non intelligam".[20] Here, Anselm is taking up a familiar theme of St. Augustine, faith as the precondition to understanding. Truth is not hidden but rather the method (modus) of arriving at it, which comes to us from God.[21] Anselm will illustrate the movement of faith to understanding by formulating a description of God, explore its possibilities, and uncover its ground.

Chapter II-IV: Demonstration Proper

God, in accordance with belief, is "something than which nothing greater can be thought": aliquid quo nihil maius cogitari possit.[22] This description of God was probably elaborated by Anselm from similar but not identical descriptions in Augustine and Boethius,[23] articulating the general notion of God's supremacy as found in the Scriptures. However this may be, Anselm proceeds to introduce the Fool of the Psalms 13, 52, who denies that God exists, and with this stratagem effects a sort of epoché, bracketing faith provisionally and taking the argument to the level of understanding. Although it proceeds from belief, this description is accepted by the Fool on the level of natural reason. The name God is given by all men to that which is above everything else.[24] The role of the Fool is essential as without his denial of God's existence the movement of the Proslogion from the second to the fifteenth chapters would be obstructed. The treatise would be simply another early Medieval devotional work. The Fool also has antecedents in Augustine. In the De Utilitate Credendi, Augustine identifies the sapientes with those who have a well formed idea of God and man, whose life and customs reflect this idea, while the remainder, whether they be erudite or ignorant, are fools (stulti).[25] Between human foolishness and Divine Truth there is human wisdom.[26] Again when Augustine presents a demonstration for the existence of God as eternal and unchangeable truth in the De Libero Arbitrio, it's point of departure is one of those fools of which Scripture writes: "The fool said in his heart: there is no God".[27]

Whatever its Augustinian roots, Anselm's use of insipiens has a peculiar characteristic. In a later work, the Cur Deus Homo, he refers to the Fool as one who maintains that something is impossible because he does not know how it occurs. But one should be satisfied if reason concludes that the reality in question exists although we do not know how. The inability to give a complete explanation of how it exists and acts does not mitigate the certitude of it's existence.[28]

The description of God as "that-than-which-a-greater-cannot-be-thought" was considered by Anselm to be truly unique, 'greater' in this context being synonymous with 'better' or 'more perfect'. It takes the hierarchy of reality (degrees of being) for granted, extending from creatures to Creator, from those beings circumscribed by space and time, and composed of parts, to that Being which is completely unfettered. This hierarchy is reflected in the noetic order and implicit in the God-description. It will also distinguish between those things whose non-existence is

18

thinkable and that whose non-existence cannot be thought.

Later interpreters have tended to ignore Anselm's strictures against Gaunilo in the Reply: the description cannot be equated with "maius omnibus", that which is greater than everything.[29] Moreover, even the word 'god' does not provide a satisfactory basis for demonstration as its meaning is at best nebulous. On the contrary, "that-than-which-a-greater-cannot-be-thought" can be understood at least to some extent and can provide a base for the argument: "is not that which is understood in some way easier to prove than that which is not understood in any way?".[30]

The Fool, when he hears "something than which nothing greater can be thought" understands what he hears and what he understands is in his mind: "et quod intelligit in intellectu eius est".[31] Anselm in his Reply against Gaunilo's objection that the description is not really understood, makes it clear that his first priority was to show that it existed in the mind in some way or other, leaving it to be determined subsequently whether it enjoys only mental existence, as fictions have, or also real existence.[32] McGill has translated in intellectu as "in relation to his understanding".[33] Not exactly a felicitous translation one must agree with him that does not refer to spatial location in the mind, "inside the human head", but rather to be "present to the human act of understanding".[34] Perhaps, the usual translation should stand. It is clearer, more familiar, and corresponds to normal patterns of speech.

The description of God (aliquid quo nihil maius cogitari possit) is in some way or another, understood by the Fool. But does he identify "something-than-which-nothing-greater-can-be-thought" with God? It really doesn't matter. All Anselm needs is that the Fool accept it as a point of departure. It is possible to contend that even should "that-than-which-nothing-greater-can-be-thought" exist in re it could still exist in a contingent manner and therefore not be a description of God. The Fool is even free to deny the existence of "something-than-which-nothing-greater-can-be-thought" just as he denied the existence of God. But he cannot deny that the description has meaning although he does not fully comprehend it: quod auditum aliquatenus intelligit.[35] Ascending from the less to the greater good anyone, the Fool included, can conjecture regarding it.[36] This is the necessary point of departure of the argument. Even though the object (illud quo) which the description refers to cannot be thought or understood, the description itself can be thought of and understood.[37] This follows on the distinction between significatio per se (meaning) and significatio per aliud (reference). For example, the word 'literate' means being literate but refers to man.[38] Believer and Fool are mediated by the description "something-than-which-nothing-greater-can-be-thought". To both

19

it has more or less the same initial meaning. It is Anselm's
task to guide the Fool from meaning to reference, from the God-
description to the affirmation of God as necessary being.

The transition from mental existence to real existence which
follows is of cardinal importance to the argument. It has been
the principal target of critics. If "that-than-which-a-greater-
cannot-be-thought" exists in the mind alone a contradiction
ensues as a greater could exist, namely it existing both in the
mind and in reality. Then, "that-than-which-a-greater-cannot-
be-thought", would be "that-than-which-a-greater-can-be-thought".
Faced by this contradiction, it follows that it exists not only
in the mind but in reality. [39]

This transition hinges on the superiority of _real_ _existence_
to _mental_ _existence_: it is greater, more perfect, better. Anselm
accepts this without hesitation and it has provided critics of
the argument with a fertile ground for protest, enthusiastically
repeated from Gaunilo to Malcolm. None the less in spite of the
many difficulties involved, it cannot be rejected out of hand.
This is a unique type of comparison, far different from those we
ordinarily make. Anselm uses the analogy of the painter and his
painting to illustrate the distinction. When the painter first
thinks of the painting he will make it exists in his understanding but not in reality, as he has yet to paint it. After it is
painted then it is both in his mind and in reality. [40]

Anselm concludes that "that-than-which-a-greater-cannot-be-
thought" exists both in the mind and in reality. Now, as all
existent things have _esse_ _in_ _intellectu_ _et_ _in_ _re_, this mode of
being is anything but privileged. If God exists, His existence
would be unique and different from all other existences, and not
subsumed under what there is. _Proslogion_ _II_ provides a sort of
half-way house which Karl Barth called God's _general_ _existence_,
"that He exists at all". [41] It should be kept in mind that the
argument in unpacking the original description of God entails
the progressive awakening of the human mind to its implications.
Proslogion _III_ is part of _one_ _single_ _argument_ not an additional
proof nor a mere 'complement' to patch up the holes left in the
second chapter. [42] A reformulation of the argument beginning with
Proslogion _III_ would, in effect, eliminate the description of
God as 'something-than-which-nothing-greater-can-be-thought' as
superfluous and center it around the possibility of a necessary
existent: if it is possible then it must actually be. [43] To do
this would invalidate Anselm's point of departure, the argument's
noetic emphasis, and his conclusion that God is something-
greater-than-can-be-thought.

Anselm overcomes the parennial temptation, Neo-Platonic in
origin, of freeing God from _what_ _there_ _is_, ultimately from exist-

ence itself: God is not being (ón) but pre-being (pro-ón). Perhaps without complete awareness of its ultimate implications, he
discovers a way in which existence can be attributed to God by
a finite mind without completely distorting either God or existence. Beginning with the is proper to mental existence, Anselm
discovers a privileged instance, "aliquid-quo-nihil-maius-
cogitari-potest", which, when expanded and unpacked, will tran-
scend what there is toward an is proper to the unknown God. In
doing this, aside from structuring the movement of the argument,
he is preparing the way for the later elaboration of analogia
entis.

The inner exigencies of "that-than-which-nothing-greater-
can-be-thought" reaches out in Proslogion III, to the very limit
of noetic possibility. Basing the argument, once again, on the
principle of contradiction, Anselm contends that it can not even
be thought not to exist.[44] He assumes that which cannot be
thought not to exist is greater than that which can be thought
not to exist. If "that-than-which-nothing-greater-can-be-thought"
could be thought not to exist, then a greater could be thought,
and a contradiction would ensue. If follows that it cannot even
be thought not to exist. Anselm bypasses the laborious ascent
from the less to the more good implicit in the description and
the possible conjectures regarding "that-than-which-a-greater-
cannot-be-thought".[45] For the first time since its original
formulation "that-than-which-a-greater-cannot-be-thought" is
identified as God: "Et hoc es tu, domine deus noster".[46]

In this way, Anselm disengages "something-than-which-a-
greater-cannot-be-thought" from mere general existence adequate
to what-there-is. After all, a being who exists merely on the
level of things would have little if any claim on divinity. God
must exist in a unique way, possess a totally singular mode of
existence. He continues the movement of Proslogion II, extending
its premise, the description of God to include the non-thinkability of its non-existence. Everything else there is, except God,
can be thought of as not existing: solus igitur verissime omnium,
et ideo maxime omnium habes esse".[47] Only God, then, truly
exists and possesses existence to the highest degree, and this is
demonstrated by a necessity encountered on the noetic level. It
illustrates, on the level of thought, the distinction between
Creator and creature, between necessary and contingent existence.
It may be well to note that the Proslogion argument, grounded in
the noetic realm, and proceeding from possibility to necessity,
is not to be equated with the argument from 'necessity and contingency' which searches for a necessary ground undergirding the
contingent existence of things.

Anselm's distinction between thinking (cogitare) and understanding (intelligere) plays an important role throughout the

21

Proslogion, indeed, throughout his works. As Michaud-Quantin has pointed out, thinking is the active side of cognition and is illustrated in the elaboration of a concept by the mind. It is a process accomplished within the field of consciousness, analogous to the eternal speaking of the WORD on the Divine level. Thinking transcends the here an now reaching the limit of noetic possibility. Understanding represents the passive element within cognition. It implies a confrontation, a permanent contact between the mind and external reality.[48] In the _Reply_, Anselm emphasizes that, unlike the opinion ascribed to Gaunilo, it is not the distinguishing characteristic of God not to be able to be understood not to exist".[49] Other things cannot be understood not to exist, viz., those that do exist. But they can _thought_ as not existing. Only God cannot be _thought_ of as not existing.[50] God's necessity extends to the very limit of thought.

While _Proslogion_ II effects the transition from mental to real existence, the third chapter moves from real to necessary existence, both aspects of one process. Objections have been raised by Malcolm with his theory of two 'ontological' argument,[51] and Charlesworth,[52] both of whom view _Proslogion_ III as a 'logically superior' proof independent of the second chapter. True enough, if we prove that God necessarily exists we prove that He really exists, but the description of God as "that-than-which-nothing-greater-can-be-thought" would disappear in the process and no substitute could possibly initiate the argument. The objections raised by Anselm against Gaunilo's substitution of "_maius omnibus_", that-which-is-greater-than-everything, apply at this juncture.[53] In addition, this would stall the argument at the third chapter and abort the further unpacking of the God-description.

The noetic horizon opened with the description of God as "something-than-which-a-greater-cannot-be-thought" extends radically into the realm of existence. That being that cannot be thought not to be is _verissime_ and _maxime esse_ and hence "_quidquid melius est esse quam non esse_", whatever it is better to be than not to be.[54] The necessary being is also a being existing _per se_, and made all things from nothing.[55] Necessary existence is the basis for distinguishing God from creatures quite different from the _per se/per aliunde_ distinction of Aquinas which opens the door to the existence of necessary creatures, for Anselm an obvious contradiction in terms.[56]

God's necessary existence is not restricted to the logical order, but is also to borrow a term from Hick, factual.[57] He is sheer, ultimate, unconditioned reality, without beginning or end, existence _semper et ubique totum_ as indicated in the _Monologion_.[58] This is substantiated by Anselm's insistence, in his _Reply_, that "that-than-which-a-greater-cannot-be-thought" is not bound by the limitations of space and time: "only that being in which there is neither beginning nor end nor conjunction of parts, and that thought does not discern save as a whole in every place and at every time, cannot be thought as not existing".[59] In brief, his reasoning is as follows: whatever exists at one place or at some time can be thought not to exist but "that-than-which-a-greater-cannot-be-thought" exists as a whole at every time and in every place and hence cannot be thought not to exist.[60] Conversely, anything with a beginning and an end or conjunction of parts can be thought not to exist.

In the Proslogion itself this point is dealt with in the thirteenth chapter: "tu solus incircumscriptus es et aeternus".[61] As that which is limited in any way by place or time is less than that which is not it follows that God exists everywhere and always, and is unlimited in a truly unique way. Distinguished from things that are wholly limited in place and time (material bodies) or partially limited (created spirits, which are wholly in one place but can be elsewhere at the same time), God is unlimited, subject neither to time nor place.[62] It follows that there are three levels: the unlimited, that which is both limited and unlimited, and the limited.

Contingent things, then, can be thought of as not existing, whether they happen to exist or not. But if they do exist, by the very fact that they do exist, they have capacity (possibility) for existence. Now this mode of possibility, as Anselm indicates in the De Casu Diaboli, is a potestas quae fit re, not potestas quae praecedit rem;[63] contingent things have no possibility to be before they are. They proceed from nothing and remain intrinsically nothing.[64] The world was nothing before it was created, in itself not even a possibility: "the world exists because God has the ability to make the world before there was a world, and not because the world itself possessed an ability to be before it was".[65]

As D.P. Henry notes, though Anselm bases himself on Boethius' distinction between antecedent and concomittant possibilities (potestas non secundum actum and potestas secundum actum), he disagrees with Boethius' example of antecedent possibility; "Socrates poterat esse cum non fuit".[66] Anselm rejects the argument that contingent beings must have existed in potentia before they are actually created. If anything had the capacity to be before it was actually created it could not have been created ex nihilo. This habit of attributing possibility to things prior to their creation arises from the imprecise use of ordinary language: "we often say 'a thing can....', not because it really can, but rather because something else can".[67] Contingent things do not possess capacity for existence except after they are created, God being the sole cause of being and possibility-to-be.

The possession of _potestas quae fit re_, distinguishes existent, contingent things from non-existent fictions. As they exist
they are possible, though existing contingently they do not have
potestas quae praecedit rem, possibility prior to existence.
This status is reflected in the noetic order by the ability to
think the non-existence of a thing. Now as 'something-than-
which-nothing-greater-can-be-thought' cannot be thought not to
exist it is separated from existent contingent things and is
possible in a way that entails necessary existence. If 'something-than-which-nothing-greater-can-be-thought' is possible (in
this unique way) then it exists, and its possibility is vouch-
safed by its noetic necessity. Hence the almost facile ease of
Anselm's statement: "_si vel cogitari potest esse, necesse est
illud esse_".[68]

This interpretation is aided by the fact that the _Proslogion_
description of God is very much in evidence in the _De Casu
Diaboli_[69] and Anselm stresses the connection between thinking
and being and their mutual exigencies. The transition is here
from possibility, reflected on the noetic level, to necessary
existence, not merely from existence in the mind to existence in
reality. _Proslogion III_ is the extension and ontological justification of _Proslogion II_ It takes for granted the peculiar
relation between possibility and necessity arising from the
doctrine of creation _ex nihilo_, the theory of _rectitudo_ as expressed in De _Veritate_, and the difficulties left in their wake.

Where does all this leave the Fool? Does he acknowledge the
existence of this necessary being or reaffirm his denial of
God's existence? Perhaps Barth is correct in stating that Anselm
has no thought of reaching an agreement with an opponent who
ignores the fear of the Lord,[70] or perhaps André Hayen's suggestion that the _Proslogion_ illustrates a "theology of conversion"[71]
should be accepted? Let us follow Anselm's explanation of the
Fool's denial of God. The question is that if God is a necessary
being and cannot be thought not to exist, how is the denial of
his existence possible? Simply because the Fool does not really
think what he is saying. He has remained on the level of mere
words (_vox_) and not advanced to the level of the reality (_res_)
they signify.[72]

Whoever really understands that God is "that-than-which-
nothing-greater-can-be-thought" also understands that not even
in thought can he not exist.[73] Recall the distinction between
significatio per se and _significatio per aliud_ previously mentioned: if the meaning of "that-than-which-nothing-greater-can-
be-thought" is understood then God _qua_ necessary being is seen
to be its reference. A denial is possible only on the assumption
that these 'words' are said "_aut sine ulla aut cum aliqua
extranea significatione_", without any signification or with some

foreign-signification.[74] The Fool's initial denial of God is
then not a statement regarding God's mode of existence but about
his own deficient mode of thought grounded on the level of mere
words.

Chapter V-XIII: The Divine Attributes

Proslogion V begins Anselm's discussion of the divine attributes further unpacking "that-than-which-nothing-greater-can-
be-thought". If God is "that-than-which-a-greater-cannot-be-
thought", He is the Supreme Good, existens per seipsum, who
made everything from nothing,[75] and is whatever it is better to be
than not to be.[76] Moreover, he is that good through which every
good exists.[77] This is precisely the second goal of the argument
as given in the preface: that God is the Supreme Good needing no
other and is He whom all things have need of for their being and
well-being. Charlesworth notes a twist given the argument by
Wyclif: because God is 'summe ens' He is also 'summe bonum', and
since it is 'more good' to exist in re et in intellectu than
merely in intellectu, God, because He is 'summe bonum', must
exist both in the mind and in reality.[78]

The original God-description is explicitly extended to the
domains of being and value fom its point of departure in the
noetic. "That-than-which-a-greater-cannot-be-thought" is
Supreme Being and Supreme good. That which from a human finite,
perspective are separate though complementary domains are in
God reduced to His simplicity and unity. The working out of the
third goal (et quaecumque de divina credimus substantia) is
reached through the principle that God is whatever it is better
to be than not to be. He is just, truthful, happy, as it is
better to be just than unjust, happy rather than unhappy, and so
forth.[79] Furthermore, as God is Supreme Good and Supreme Being
no perfection can be lacking in Him. The following chapters
extend this principle to encompass additional divine attributes.

Although it is true that only the first stage of the argument, comprising only three out of twenty-six chapters, has
given Anselm a place in the history of philosophy, it has also
most probably contributed to the depredations which the argument
as a whole has suffered. As certain chapters simply carry out a
lengthy and at times thematically uninteresting unpacking of
"that-than-which-nothing-greater-can-be-thought" into the domain
of the divine attributes they can reasonably be omitted but it is
really surprising that even a careful exegete such as Charlesworth
simply omits Proslogion XIV, vital to the understanding of the
argument, and sums up the last eleven chapters by reciting the
concluding prayer.[80] Other scholars have omitted entire chapters
from the text itself, probably considering them to be philosophi-

cally valueless.[81] This should not be condoned unless one is content with a truncated argument and consequently a somewhat mangled interpretation.

Chapter XIV-XIX: The Quest For Experience

The question which initiates _Proslogion_ XIV ushers in a new dimension of the argument: "An invenisti, anima mea, quod quaerebas"?[82] God has been found, true enough: He is the highest of all, "that-than-which-a-better-cannot-be-thought," life itself, light, wisdom, goodness....who exists everywhere and always. This has been understood, "tam certa veritate et vera certitudine", with certain truth and true certitude.[83] Anselm does not for a moment doubt the efficacy of his reasoning: the existence of God has been demonstrated. Still, this demonstration is confined to the cognitive order and has yet to overflow into experience: "Si vero invenisti: quid est, quod non sentis quod invenisti".[84] If God has been found why is he not experienced? This plaint which evokes the anguish of the first chapter becomes a theme that runs through _Proslogion_ XVII - XVIII. God is hidden from a soul whose 'senses' have been hardened, dulled, and obstructed through vetustus languor peccati, the ancient weakness of sin.[85] The soul 'listens', 'tastes', 'smells, and 'feels', but God is not experienced. Anselm's insistence on the sorrow and confusion that this lack of experience generates, his presumption that the experience of God's presence is to be expected, and his repetition of the joy/anguish dichotomy, point to the unfinished character of the argument. After all, man was created in order to see God, as Anselm indicates in _Proslogion_ I.[86] The prayer of the eighteenth chapter reflects this aspiration: "purify, heal, sharpen, illumine the eye of my soul so that it may see you".[87] In a manner reminiscent of Plato's analogies of the sun and the cave in the _Republic_ (VI,VII), and Augustine's parallel texts,[88] Anselm now contrasts the 'light and truth' requisite for understanding and this 'light and truth' in itself, i.e., God. Nothing can be understood without 'lux tua et veritas tua' and God is known in a fragmentary and partial manner (aliquatenus).[89] Any further progress in vision is impeded both by the weakness of the soul and the fullness (amplitudo) and splendor of God. Truths are many while that light, "de qua micat omne verum quod rationali menti lucet",[90] (from which shines every truth that gives light to the understanding), is pure and simple. As weak eyes see by the light of the sun and yet cannot look directly at the sun itself so the mind cannot attain the 'inaccessible light' in which God dwells, dazzled as it is by its splendour and overwhelmed by its immensity.[91] Prayer is the logical recourse.

This transition from the horizontal level of understanding, grounded on the divine light to the vertical level of the divine light itself, is introduced by Proslogion XV. As it is possible to think that there is a being, "a-greater-than-can-be-thought", then God must be it.[92] If He were not then God would not be "that-than-which-a-greater-cannot-be-thought", as a greater, viz., "a-greater-than-can-be-thought" could be thought. The principle of self-contradiction again does yeoman service. God is greater than any notion we can possibly have of Him. In the Monologion, Anselm had indicated that it is impossible to speak of God directly, but only through a similitude or image.[93] The original description of God as "something-than-which-nothing-greater-can-be-thought" can then be considered a formula for obtaining similitudes not a strict definition. In the Reply, Anselm distinguishes (as he does in Proslogion IV) between understanding the verbal formulation of the God-description and the object to thich it refers: "there is no doubt at all that what is heard can be thought of and understood even if the thing itself cannot be thought of and understood".[94] In this way both the cogency of the argument's approach to God and His transcendent reality are safeguarded.

Chapter XX-XXVI: Adumbration of Beatitude

The remaining chapters center on the unity and the goodness of this inaccessible God. Chapters eighteen to twenty-one stress unity, twenty-three to twenty-five, goodness, with Proslogion XXII providing the bridge connecting them. He is "ipsa unitas, nullo intellecto divisibilis", unity itself, indivisible by any mind,[95] in whom all attributes are identified, existing as a whole everywhere and always,[96] possessing an eternity which includes those 'eternal' things whose being is parcelled out in time.[97] Only God exists in a strict and absolute (proprie et simpliciter) manner as only He enjoys eternally present existence and cannot be thought not to exist.[98] God is the one and supreme Good,[99] the 'unus necessarius' of Luke's Gospel.

Interspersed throughout the Proslogion are exhortations to 'lift the soul' and a 'rouse the mind': "rouse and lift up your whole understanding (totus intellectus tuus) and think as much as you can on what kind (quale) and how great (quantum) this good is".[100] Anselm does this by ascending from the 'less good' to the 'more good' in the manner prescribed by the Reply, using those things than which something greater can be thought as the point of departure for conjecture about "that-than-which-a-greater-cannot-be-thought".[101] Created life becomes a spring board to creative life, wisdom in the knowledge of things to Wisdom creative of things, joy in particular goods to joy in a

Good that contains the joyfulness of all goods: "not (a joy) such
as we have experienced in created things, but as different from
this as the Creator differs from the creature".[102] The emphasis
is displaced from the speculation regarding the Divine attributes
to possible human participation in the Divine life.

A rather lengthy excursus follows regarding the state of the
blessed, i.e., those who will enjoy the Supreme Good. Anselm
presents a long string of Scriptural citations, the majority from
the Psalms, Matthew, and Paul, ensconced in a lyrical outpouring
which celebrates the beatific life. The blessed will rejoice in
proportion to their love with their whole heart, mind, and
soul,[103] joy which is "plenum, et plus quam plenum", complete and
more than complete.[104] The life which will be made complete in
beatitude is already being lived. Knowledge and love will grow
'here' and be made complete 'there'. Here, joy is great in hope
(in spe), there it will be complete in reality (in re).[105] This
unique joy, as different as is the Creator from the creature, is
not experienced at present but is discovered as a future possibility, consequent on growth in love and knowledge. The possibility of this unique joy is now operative though actual fruition
is postponed.

This unique joy is the privileged experience that Anselm
aspired to, one through which God is manifested. Anselm's
insistent prayer for 'gaudium et laetitia' has been answered, not
by the experience itself, but by hopeful anticipation of it. The
Proslogion Argument, complete on its own level, that of faith
which seeks and obtains understanding, is fulfilled eschatologi-
cally:

> 'God of truth, I ask that I may receive
> so that my 'joy may be complete! Until
> then let my mind meditate on it, let my
> tongue speak of it, let my heart love it,
> let my mouth preach it. Let my soul hunger
> for it, let my flesh thirst for it, my whole
> being desire it, until I enter into the 'joy
> of the Lord' (Matt. xxv, 21), who is God, Three
> in one, 'blessed forever. Amen', (Rom.i,25)[106]

NOTES

1. The text is the Schmitt critical edition, _S. Anselmi_, _Opera Omnia_ (Edinburgi: Thomam Nelson et Filios, 1946-1961), 6 Vols. _Proslogion_, Vol. I, _prooem._, 93, 10-13.

2. Eadmer, _De Vita Sancti Anselmi_, 26.

3. _Proslogion_, _prooem._, 93, 16-19.

4. _Vita_, _Loc. cit._ We must note, however, that Eadmer had no first hand acquaintance with Anselm's activities until his arrival in England in 1092. Refer to F.S. Schmitt, "Zur Chronologie der Werke des hl. Anselm von Canterbury", in _Revue Benedictine_, 44 (1932), pp. 322-350.

5. _Proslogion_, _prooem._, 93, 6-9.

6. '_Argumentum_' can mean a single premise in a process of reasoning, a train of reasoning considered as a whole, or the principal reason for accepting a conclusion. For the latter refer to the _Responsio_, in which he addresses Gaunilo as follows: "_Quod quam falsum sit_, _fide et conscientia tua pro firmissimo utor argumento._", _Opera_, I, 130, 15-16.

7. _Proslogion_, _prooem._, 93, 9-10.

8. To wit, that God is whatever it is better to be than not to be. _Proslogion_, V, 104, 15-16. _Responsio_, (x), 139, 3-4.

9. _Proslogion_, _prooem._, 93, 21-94, 2.

10. _Epistola de Incarnatione Verbi_, (_Opera_, Vol. II), VI, 20, 16-21.

11. _Why God Became Man_, Trans. and notes by J. Colleran (Albany: Magi Books, 1969), p. 235, note 139.

12. R. W. Southern, _Saint Anselm and his Biographer_ (Cambridge: C.U.P., 1963), p. 47.

13. _Proslogion_, I, 100, 12-13.

14. _Ibid._, 98, 14-51.

15. _Ibid._, 100, 13-15.

16. <u>Ibid.</u>, 100, 8-10.

17. <u>Ibid.</u>, 97, 7-10.

18. The difference is also obvious. Anselm wishes to speak to God, Descartes to know himself. See <u>The Philosophical Works of Descartes</u>, ed. Haldane and Ross (London: Cambridge University Press, 1967), Vol. I, p. 157. At the beginning of the Third meditation, Descartes states: "I shall now close my eyes, I shall stop my ears, I shall call away all my senses, I shall even efface from my thoughts all the images of corporeal things, or at least ----- I shall esteem them as vain and false; and thus holding converse only with myself and considering my own nature, I shall try little by little to reach a better knowledge of and a more familiar acquaintanceship with myself."

19. <u>Proslogion</u>, IV, 103, 16-19.

20. <u>Ibid.</u>, I, 100, 18-19.

21. See especially <u>De Utilitate Credendi</u>, 8, 20.

22. <u>Proslogion</u>, II, 101, 5-6.

23. See ample editor's notes, <u>Opera Omnia</u>, I, p. 102, note line 3. Charlesworth believes that the immediate source of this 'formula' is to be found in St. Augustine. <u>St. Anselm's Proslogion</u>, Trans., intro., phil. commentary by M. J. Charlesworth (Oxford: Claredon Press, 1965), p. 56. This work reprints the critical edition of the Latin Text, along with the English Translation.

24. <u>Monologion</u>, I, 86, 17-22.

25. <u>Op. cit.</u>, 12, 27.

26. <u>Ibid.</u>, 13, 33.

27. <u>Op. cit.</u>, II, 2, 5.

28. <u>Op. cit.</u>, I, 25, (<u>Opera Omnia</u>, II), 96, 2-3. Also refer to <u>Monologion</u>, ch. 64, (<u>Opera Omnia</u>, I), 74, 30-75, 16. Here he expresses the opinion that one who is investigating an incomprehensible subject-matter, such as the Holy Trinity, ought to be satisfied if his reason takes him far enough to recognize that this reality actually exists.

29. Responsio, I, (V), 134, 24-136, 2. Anselm's reasoning here
    is (1) the two descriptions ('that-than-which-nothing-
    greater-can-be-thought' and 'that-which-is-greater-than-
    everything') are not equivalent, as it is not evident that
    "that-which-is-greater-than-everything" cannot be thought
    not to exist; (2) for Gaunilo's formulation to be demonstra-
    tive he would just have to show that 'that-which-is-greater-
    than-everything' is to be equated with 'that-than-which-
    nothing-greater-can-be-thought'. At best, then, Gaunilo's
    formulation would require an additional inference, while the
    Proslogion formulation is self-sufficing.

30. Ibid., (VII), 136, 30,-137, 5.

31. Proslogion, II, 101, 7-9.

32. Responsio (VI), 136, 3-10.

33. The Many-Faced Argument, edited by J. Hick and A. C. McGill
    (New York: MacMillan Co., 1967), pp. 4-6. Esp. p. 5,
    note 10.

34. Idem.- To be candid I have never seen 'in intellectu'
    interpreted as "inside the human head" but let us allow
    McGill his point.

35. Responsio (VII), 136, 30-137, 5.

36. This follows from Proslogion V where God is considered as
    being describable as "quidquid melius est esse quam non
    esse", 104, 16. In the Responsio, "Quoniam namque omne
    minus bonum in tantum est simile maiori bono inquantum est
    bonum: patet cuilibet rationabili menti, quia de bonis
    minoribus ad maiora conscendendo ex iis quibus aliquid maius
    cogitari potest, multum possumus conicere illud quo nihil
    potest maius cogitari". (VIII),137, 14-18. Also ff.

37. Ibid., (IX), 138, 4-6. In the same way as 'ineffable' or
    'inconceivable' can be thought and understood, even though
    the thing referred to cannot be thought of and understood.
    Ibid., 7ff.

38. See especially Desmond P. Henry, The De Grammatico of St.
    Anselm (Notre Dame: University of Notre Dame Press, 1964),
    p. 110, No. 5.320.

39. Proslogion, II, 101, 15-102, 3.

40. Ibid., II, 101, 9-13.

41. Barth, op. cit., Eng. trans., Anselm: Fides Quaerens Intellectum (Cleveland: Meridian Books, 1962), p. 129, note 2.

42. Malcolm contends that Proslogion III is, in effect, a second ontological argument. The first is Proslogion II and is fallacious as it rests on the 'false doctrine' that existence is a perfection. The second, however, is grounded on the logical impossibility of non-existence as a perfection and is acceptable. 'Anselm's Ontological Arguments' in The Philosophical Review, LXIX, No. 1 (Jan. 1960), pp. 41-62. Charlesworth believes that it is possible to reconstruct Proslogion III on Leibnizian lines to make it more 'economical' and rigorous by doing away with the definition of God as 'that-than-which-nothing-greater-can-be-thought'. St. Anselm's Proslogion, p. 74, note 2.

43. This suggestion is Charlesworth's, op. cit., p. 73ff.

44. Proslogion, III, 102, 8-103, 2.

45. Refer to note 36.

46. Proslogion, III, 103, 3-4.

47. Ibid., 103, 7-11.

48. "Notes sur le vocabulaire psychologique de saint Anselme", in Spicilegium Beccense, pp. 23-30, esp. pp. 24-25.

49. Responsio (IV), 133, 27ff.

50. Idem.

51. See note 42.

52. Idem.

53. As indicated in note 28, 'Maius-omnibus' and 'quo-maius-cogitari-non-potest' are not equivalent. Anselm's main contention is that it may be objected that 'maius-omnibus' though existing may be thought of as non existing and that something greater can be thought although it does not exist. An additional inference would then be needed, one which would conclude to 'quo-maius-cogitari-non-possit'. For full weight of the argument see Responsio (V), 134, 24-136, 2.

54. Proslogion, V, 104, 14-17.

55. Ibid., V, 104, 11-13.

56. For Anselm the basis for distinguishing God from His creatures is necessity/contingency; for Aquinas the per se/per
aliud distinction. A good case for the existence of
necessary creatures in St. Thomas has been made, based on
the Tertia Via, by Dermot O'Donoghue: "An Analysis of the
Tertia Via of St. Thomas" in The Irish Theological Quarterly
20 (1953), 135-140. In this case, as Hopkins and Richardson
point out, "a necessary being, like a contingent being, has
its being and its ability to be (or its inability not to be)
only from God, and not per se. But if God were to remove
His creative powers from the necessary creature, then the
resultant "state" would be truly nothing, for a necessary
creature has no modal status spart from the creative activity
of God Himself - who alone exists per se". Anselm of
Canterbury: Truth, Freedom, and Evil (New York: Harper and
Row, 1967), p. 53. See also, Jasper Hopkins, A Companion to
the Study of St. Anselm (Minneapolis: University of Minnesota
Press, 1972), p. 80.

57. John Hick, "God as Necessary Being", in The Journal of
Philosophy, Vol. 57, Nos. 22-23, p. 730ff.

58. Note especially Monologion, XXI, 36, 6-38, 27.

59. Responsio, IV , 134, 4-6; also I , 131, 2-5; 131, 18-132,
2; III , 133, 15-20; also in the Proslogion, especially
chapters XIII, XIX, and XXI.

60. Idem.

61. Proslogion, XIII, 110, 15.

62. Ibid., 110, 16-111, 3.

63. De Casu Diaboli, (Opera I), XII, 252, 23-26.

64. Ibid., 253, 4-6. I.233, 8-11.

65. Ibid., 253, 13-17.

66. Patrologia Latina, Vol. 64, 381 B-C, noted by D. P. Henry,
Remarks on St. Anselm's Treatment of Possibility', in
Spicilegium Beccense, p. 19, note 2.

67. Ibid., 253, 19-24. Hopkins notes that in these texts Anselm
uses the Latin word potestas to express both capacity and
possibility. Op. cit., p. 178.

68. Responsio, I, 131, 1-2.

69. De Casu Diaboli, IV, 241, 29-242, 6.

70. Barth, op. cit., p. 104ff.

71. André Hayen, "The Role of the Fool in St. Anselm and the
    Necessarily Apostolic Character of True Christian Reflection"
    in The Many-Faced Argument, pp. 165; 169.

72. Proslogion, IV, 103, 18-20.

73. Ibid., 103, 20-104, 4.

74. Ibid., 104, 1-2.

75. Ibid., V. 104, 11-13.

76. Ibid., 104, 15-16.

77. Ibid., 104, 14-15.

78. St. Anselm's Proslogion, p. 60, note 2.

79. Proslogion, V, 104, 15-16.

80. "The remaining chapters of the Proslogion consider the
    inaccessibility and the goodness of God...", op. cit., p. 82.

81. This is true of even men like Plantinga and Hick. The
    latter states that "the ontological argument is to be found
    in chapters 2-4 of Anselm's Proslogion." Philosophy of
    Religion (Englewood Cliffs: Prentice-Hall,Inc., 1963), p. 15,
    note 1. Plantinga also reproduces only Proslogion II-IV,in
    The Ontological Argument (Garden City: Doubleday & Co., Inc.,
    1965), edited by him and Richard Taylor.

82. Proslogion, XIV, III, 8.

83. Ibid., III, 11-13.

84. Ibid., III, 13-15.

85. Ibid., XVII, 113, 12-15.

86. "Denique ad te videndum factus sum, et nondum feci propter
    quod factus sum" Proslogion, I, 98, 14-15.

87. Ibid., XVIII, 114, 11-13.

88. De Genesi ad Litteram, XII, 31, 59, De Trinitate, XIV, 15, 21; IX, 6, 9; IX, 6, 11; De Civitate Dei, XI, 27, 2; et al. The possible influence of Augustine's theory of 'illumination' on the Proslogion will be discussed in chapter III of the present study.

89. Proslogion, XIV, 111, 18-21.

90. Ibid., 112, 5-11.

91. Ibid., XVI, 112, 21-27.

92. Ibid., XV, 112, 14-17.

93. Monologion, chapters LXV and LXVI. LXV, 76, 11-18. et at.

94. Responsio, IX , 138, 4-11.

95. Proslogion, XVIII, 114, 22-24.

96. Ibid., 114, 25-115, 4.

97. Ibid., XX, 115, 26-116, 3.

98. Ibid., XXII, 116, 22ff.

99. Ibid., 116, 22-117, 2.

100. Ibid., XXIV, 117, 25-26.

101. Responsio, VIII , 137, 14-18.

102. Proslogion, XXIV, 118, 2-3.

103. Ibid., XXV, 118, 12-120, 20. Especially 120, 17-20.

104. Ibid., XXVI, 120, 25-121, 1.

105. Ibid., 121, 14-18.

106. Ibid., 121, 21-122, 2.

CHAPTER III

FAITH AND REASON

The initial title of the Proslogion was Fides quaerens intellectum. It summarizes not only the expectations of the argument but the difficulties encountered in exegesis since Gaunilo wrote his Pro Insipiente. The temptation to credit Anselm with views that are not his own, to foist these conceptions on the Proslogion to interpret it in their light has often proven to be an insuperable temptation. The necessary antidote is to place Anselm in the context of Medieval thought and the Proslogion in the context of Anselm's thought. A discussion of his conception of reason and faith is a good starting point.

Although a set conception of reason and faith is presupposed by all of Anselm's works and valuable clues are to be found in his earlier works, it is in his works and letters written after 1090 that it can be examined in detail. Perhaps the reason for the problem surfacing is due to Anselm finding himself in a rather embarrassing position: it was rumored that his views on the Trinity-as well as those of his teacher Lanfranc, Archbishop of Canterbury- were similar to those of Roscelin. Although very little is known about the theories of Roscelin, we do know from Anselm's correspondence that he was accused of maintaining that the three divine persons are either three things or the Father and Holy Spirit became incarnate together with the Son.[1] As each horn of the dilemma is flagrantly heretical to be linked with an advocate of such dangerous views was, to say the least, undesirable. A brief but illuminating defense against this accusation is given in a letter to Bishop Fulco of Beauvais (Epistola 136). Refuting the charge, Anselm concurs in Roscelin's condemnation. Let him remain anathema as long as he persists in his obstinacy. He is not a Christian at all.[2]

Anselm makes a distinction between the 'Christian' and the 'impious.' It is completely out of the question to "throw back into uncertainty" those things established on "solid rock" at the behest of a person who lacks understanding. The Christian must be held to the pledge taken at baptism. Still, Christian faith can be defended by reason against the impious: "it should be shown rationally that they irrationally despise us."[3] A believer should progress through faith to understanding--the leitmotiv of the Proslogion--and be delighted when he can reach understanding. If he cannot let him revere what he is unable to

understand.[4] The Christian is given an exhortation, the unbeliever an argument. It is significant that in this text the
Christian who reneges from his faith, as Roscelin presumably did,
is taken to task as lacking <u>understanding</u>.

Epistola de Incarnatione Verbi

At about this time Anselm began a work against Roscelin
which developed into the <u>Epistola</u> <u>de</u> <u>Incarnatione</u> <u>Verbi</u> (1092-4)
in which his views on faith and reason are presented. He gives
four prerequisites to knowledge necessary before applying human
judgment to the 'deep things' of faith: (1) the cleansing of
the heart by faith; (2) the enlightening of the eyes by keeping
the precepts of the Lord; (3) humble obedience to God; and (4)
putting aside the flesh to live according to the spirit.[5] The
believer may now engage in the quest for the reasons why his
faith is true. The <u>fides</u> in quest of <u>intellectus</u> is bound to
preconditions, a type of musiké, which purifies the mind for the
task of attaining knowledge. According to Anselm there is a
correlation between knowledge of the Scriptures and the quest for
understanding: "the more richly we are fed on those things in
Sacred Scripture which nourish us through obedience, the more
deeply we are carried on to those things which satisfy them
through understanding."[6]

At least insofar as the Christian is concerned, Anselm makes
a distinction between <u>what</u> is known and <u>how</u> it is known. If the
necessary preconditions are not complied with then the correct
order (as prescribed in Isaiah 7:9)[7] is inverted and errors are
committed. This inversion may even result in the loss of faith,[8]
and error is possible because of defective understanding.[9]
Belief precedes understanding because it provides the requisite
'<u>alae</u> <u>spirituales</u>' (spiritual wings) for reason to operate effec-
tively. Faith establishes reason solidly within the domain of
its proper operations. It generates clarity of intellectual
vision that prevents the believer from becoming a 'heretic of
dialectic' which is to say a nominalism as attributed to
Roscelin: those whose minds are so covered over by corporeal
images that they cannot extricate themselves from them, "confused and complicated by a multiplicity of images."[10] Mere
sounds (<u>flatus</u> <u>vocis</u>) are identified with substances, colors not
distinguished from material objects, nor human wisdom from the
individual soul.[11]

It does not seem that Anselm is adding to the position taken
by Augustine in De <u>Utilitate</u> <u>Credendi</u>, and discussed previously.
Belief is a prerequisite to understanding[12] as it gives us the
method (<u>modus</u>), previously hidden, to arrive at truth.[13]

38

Nurtured in belief, truth can be understood and possessed if the believer has a simple spirit and is purified by an ordered style of life.[14] The spirit is prepared by faith to receive the 'seed of truth' and by a purification of life and customs is disposed to accept reason.[15] This, it will be remembered, is the work in which Augustine compares the Fool to the Wise, equating the latter with those who possess a "well-formed" idea of God which is reflected in their lives and customs.[16]

Both Anselm and Augustine are here following a speculative current that finds its Christian expression in Matthew, V, 8, "Blessed are the clean of heart; they shall see God" The contrast between Christianity and Paganism is not that purification of reason is necessary--it is found in antiquity from Plato to the Corpus Hermeticum--but that it is a gift of God. Perhaps the best example is found in Justin Martyr's Dialogue with Trypho in which he describes his own spiritual pilgrimage: Stoic, Peripatetic, Pythagorean, Platonist, then Christian. On one of his walks by the sea he speaks to an old man who asks him, "Is it possible for the mind of man to see God at any time, if it is uninstructed by the Holy Spirit?" Justin, then a Platonist, replies: "Yes, if the mind is pure." He bases his answer on the fundamental kinship between the human and the divine. But his questioner insists that the human soul is mortal and has no kinship with the divine. Man must be 'instructed' by the Holy Spirit.[17] Following the text we find basically the same position as Anselm, faith is the necessary propeudeutic to the vision of God while understanding becomes the midpoint between them: ad videndum deum purgandus animus.

Returning to the Epistola, Anselm insists that if the intellect is not confused by a multiplicity of images (as those 'heretics of dialectic') it will be evident that the simple is superior to the composite. Everything composite can be divided either in reality or in thought, but the same is not true of what is simple: "no intellect can dissolve into parts anything whose parts are incapable of being apprehended by thought."[18] If God is thought of as composed of parts then a greater being can be thought and this is impossible.[19] As God exists always and everywhere divisibility is totally alien to Him. The being and power of God are identical "a nature which is above everything, free from every law of space, time, and composition."[20] The unity of God is affirmed at the expense of Roscelin's imputed tritheism. God is, in Anselm's view, nothing less than "Simple Eternity Itself," a perfect unity, comparable to a point within a point.[21] A point, like eternity, is simple, without parts, and indivisible. A point added to a point, no space intervening, makes only one point. Eternity added to eternity makes only one and the same eternity.

This ongoing debate with a hypothetical opponent for whom
Anselm provides an argument halts momentarily when he refers to
previous works touching on the same theme. Both the Monologion
and the Proslogion are mentioned as designed to show that it is
possible to prove by necessary reasons, apart from Scriptural
authority, those things which "we hold by faith concerning the
divine nature and the persons, except the Incarnation."[22] In
both treatises, Anselm indicates he was replying to those who,
while unwilling to believe what they do not understand, deride
those who do believe and also to assist the efforts of those who
humbly seek to understand what they already believe.[23]

Anselm returns to the attitude indicated in Epistola 136
to Bishop Fulco: rational argumentation against the impious, a
call to obedience to the renegade, an advance from faith to
understanding for the believer. As we have seen, the Proslogion
deals with both the 'impious' (The Fool) and the believer. The
unbeliever is refuted by means of necessary reasons and the
believer aided in the understanding of his belief. The
Proslogion has both a religious and a philosophical aspect, both
directed to the fullest possible knowledge of God. It is both
demonstration and meditation.

De Concordia

But what of reason unaided by faith? Can it arrive at truth
by itself or must it be converted by the 'fides' that is
'quaerens intellectum?' This is basically the problem of the
Fool in the Proslogion. Is he, (1) merely controverted by
Anselm, i.e., convicted of foolishness, (2) convinced by Anselm's
argument on a rational level without accepting faith, or (3)
converted to belief in God? Barth, grounded in Calvinist theology, opts for the first solution,[24] Charlesworth seems to incline
towards the second,[25] and André Hayen towards the third.[26]
During his last years Anselm wrote a treatise (De Concordia)
which extends and amplifies the position he took in his letter
to Bishop Fulco and the Epistola de Incarnatione Dei. The full
title of the treatise reflects the perspective from which Anselm's
speculations are made: On the Harmony of the Foreknowledge, the
Predestination, and the Grace of God with Free Choice.

The sixth chapter of the De Concordia contains remarks on
St. Paul's dictum of Romans 10, that faith comes by hearing.
Anselm indicates that prior to faith there must be some degree
of understanding, that there is a knowing which precedes as well
as one that follows faith. The word of God must be understood
before it can be believed, and understood correctly. At a far
remove from any Kierkegaard-like 'leap of faith,' Anselm compares

the meaning of the word of God to a <u>seed</u> that must be laboriously cultivated.[27] To will uprightly--more will be said about <u>rectitude</u> presently--is necessary for salvation but it is impossible to will without previously having understood.[28]

Although knowing does not generate faith there is no faith without previous knowing: "faith comes into being when, by grace, rectitude of willing is added to the conception... then a man believes what he hears."[29] The 'seed' is planted by hearing, is understood, and grows through rectitude of the will, given by God.[30] However, not all 'seeds' germinate. Knowing does not generate faith but only makes it possible.

The weakening of man through original sin is reflected in the debilitation of the will. Faith comes about when rectitude of the will is added to knowing and knowing is the product of hearing. The 'sound of the word' conveys a meaning and this, as has been indicated, is the 'seed' out of which faith <u>may</u> arise. This knowing is prior to faith as "no one can believe what he does not first know in his heart."[31] Before a man believes he must know what should be believed. The existence of a type of knowledge prior to belief which does not necessarily issue in belief helps to explain the enigma of the Fool in the <u>Proslogion</u>. He disappears from the scene in <u>Proslogion</u> IV even though the demonstration, as far as Anselm is concerned, has been understood with '<u>certa veritate et vera certitudine</u>.'[32] But this pertains to the intellect not the will, the 'seed' of meaning not the rectitude of will necessary for faith. As this rectitude be given only by God the outcome has to be left in obscurity.

If there is both a knowing before faith and one generated by faith both of which may be true, what separates the believer from the unbeliever? Anselm does not fall into a quandry in which he has either to deny the validity of knowledge before faith, which is to say, the efficacy of reason, or to deny the efficacy of faith as the point of departure for reason. He affirms both and in doing so gives the lie to the fideistic and rationalistic interpretations of his thought. He holds on to both horns of the dilemma and affirms that reason is, to some extent, capable of understanding even the things of God prior to faith though it is faith which guides reason in its earthly pilgrimage to its source. The believer can enter into discussion with the unbeliever, both parties accepting the 'rules of the game' dictated by reason, while at the same time, guiding himself to a more profound understanding of his faith.

Cur Deus Homo

Perhaps it would be instructive to turn to the Cur Deus Homo, the 'fundamental treatise',[33] to further investigate Anselm's position on faith and reason. In the commendatio he explicitly states that in this life, understanding is the mean between faith and direct vision: "I consider that the more one advances towards understanding the closer he approaches the direct vision we all eagerly desire."[34] He insists that understanding is not a pious expectation but a spiritual exigency. With an eye on the exaggerated 'spiritualists' of his day such as Peter Damien, Anselm insists that no one ought to be reprehended if after having been confirmed in the faith he desires to investigate its meaning.[35] Investigation has no limit as unlimited truth cannot be fully comprehended by the human mind.[36] As through understanding man rises towards the vision of God, it is not merely allowed to the believer but, given the proper disposition, is required of him: "as right order requires that we believe the profound truths of the Christian faith before we presume to analyze them by reason, so it would seem to be a matter of negligence if after we have been confirmed in the faith, we make no effort to understand what we believe."[37]

Anselm's conception of original sin and redemption is germane at this point. Mankind, because of original sin lost rectitude of the will, a loss which cannot be remedied through his own efforts. The Incarnation effects a "humana restauratio," a restoration of the right order of things. This makes it possible for man, through faith, to regain this lost rectitude of the will which is the precondition for the intellect to be properly ordered to God. It restores to reason the integrity which was lost by the fall and establishes the proper correlation between the knowledge of God, self-knowledge, and spiritual perfection. To put it in another way, faith directs reason towards its transcendent goal.

As indicated there is an exercise of reason prior to faith which is its 'seed'; if it is germinated through grace then reason is enabled to move towards a more profound understanding of God, not merely as an object of knowledge but as the end of all existence. Following the proper order (credo ut intelligam) it is exempt from the possibilities of error mentioned previously. It cannot be denied that the 'infideles' labor under restrictions which have been overcome by the believers, but one of these is assuredly not a reason totally obfuscated by the Fall.[38] Anselm considered that the unbeliever, as well as the believer, possessed a reason only weakened by the fall and capable of arriving at truth. The Cur Deus Homo itself was expressly written to convince 'sola ratione' --by reason alone-- that it was necessary for God to become man, a theme rather far afield of what usually would be considered strictly philosophical.[39] He advises the believer to ponder the objections of the unbelievers: "although they, of course, seek arguments of reason because they do not believe, while we seek them because we do believe, what we are seeking is, nevertheless, one and the same."[40] The Proslogion sets out to demonstrate the existence of God in the face of opposition from the Fool and this presupposes a common ground. If the Fool were unable to understand the description of God, to make distinctions, or to apprehend logical argument, the treatise would merely be a rather curious exercise in fulility.

Karl Barth

Before continuing this study it may be well to stop and examine Karl Barth's views which provide a rather serious obstacle to the present interpretation. To begin with, Barth is perfectly correct in assuming that Anselm is not attempting to provide faith with a rational justification. It is not the existence of faith but rather the nature of faith that requires knowledge.[41] In Anselm's opinion it is presumptuous to attempt to ground faith on reason. It would be like trying to support Mount Olympus with pegs and ropes.[42] True faith, if 'living', will demand an expansion into understanding. Only 'dead faith' is self-satisfied and does not seek knowledge.[43] In Barth's words, faithful to Anselm, "just because we possess the certainly of faith, we must hunger after the fidei ratio."[44] Again, his contention that what is right should be rightly believed,[45] duly mirrors the stipulations of the Epistola de Incarnatione Verbi, and his view that the 'decisive capacity' for the intellectus fidei does not belong to autonomous human reason but has to be bestowed on it[46] cannot be faulted. Only God can germinate the 'seed' of meaning, and this is a matter concerning the will-- to believe rightly what is true--not primarily a matter of intellect.

Barth insists that there is a 'gulf' between believer and unbeliever over which agreement is impossible, that all discussion with the insipiens is 'pointless and meaningless' as he is beyond all help.[47] This opinion must have appeared as rather weak to Barth himself, contradicting as it does the stated purpose of the Proslogion. He attempts to explain this effort of Anselm to engage the Fool as a pious wish: he addresses the unbeliever as a believer trusting not in his lack of faith but rather in his faith.[48] Perhaps Barth was forced into this position by his fear that a common ground between believer an unbe-

liever would imply the possibility of beginning the quaerens
intellectum with merely the rules of autonomous human reason and
the data of human experience, creating a sort of 'shadow credo,'.[49] But reason provides no link between the believer and the
unbeliever. Either the unbeliever is in error or an autonomous
reason capable of constructing a rational 'faith' is possible.
However, this is not so as ultimately it is proper willing that
distinguishes the believer,not reason as contrasted to unreason.
Faith is not, as Barth believes, an alien force which subjects
reason to its imperatives but rather a 'seedbed' containing the
'deeper reasons' of things which prompts reason to be faithful
to its own exigencies.[50]

Perhaps an analogy from the field of psychoanalysis is op-
portune. It is not sufficient to discover unconscious material
and communicate it to the patient as this 'knowledge' is thera-
peutically neutral. It a must be found at the place where it
became unconscious owing to repression. The repression must
first be eliminated and then the substitution of the conscious
for the unconscious material can proceed smoothly. Only then
does this knowledge have therapeutic value.[51] In an analogous
manner it is only when right willing is added to right thinking
that knowledge becomes 'therapeutic,' i.e., directed to the
ultimate vision of God. Nevertheless, the initial knowledge,
whether of the patient or the unbeliever, is precisely the very
same knowledge which, when the additional factor is added, is
capable of transforming him psychologically or spiritually.
This is the privileged understanding that arises from faith.

As Scripture opposes no truth and favors no falsity it exercises censorship over reason although "when Holy Scripture either
affirms clearly or does not deny what reason teaches, it contains
the authority for all the truth that reason apprehends."[52] This
is a remarkable statement. A conclusion accepted on the basis
of clear reason and not contradicted by Scripture is supported
by its authority. In De Processione Spiritus Sancti defending
the filioque against the Greeks, Anselm expects his adversaries
to be led rationally from that which they confess without hesitation to that which they do not as yet accept.[53] The Latins had
not, as the Greeks thought, corrupted the Credo by this addition
but only added something new.[54] In another brief apologetical
work directed against the same quarter (Epistola de Sacrificio
Azimi et Fermentati)--this time the charge was against the Latin
practice of using unleavened bread in the Eucharist-- Anselm
concludes by pointing out that whatever is done against reason
and without authority is to be repudiated.[55]

Rectitude

Anselm's methodology in the above apologetical works sheds
some light on those treatises, like the Proslogion, Monologion
and the Cur Deus Homo, in which he expressly brackets articles
of faith and proceeds 'sola ratione.'[56] As both faith and reason
are rooted in God, they complement rather than oppose each other
in man's search for fullness of truth. In order to fully appre-
ciate the implications involved a few remarks on Anselm's theory
of rectitude are pertinent especially as it may be viewed, as
Dom Pouchet does, as 'le centre vital où se nouent la pensée et
la action."[57] God is Supreme Rectitude in that He is who He is
and what He should be, the ultimate principle of being and intelligibility, the law of creation. Anselm, following Christian
belief, stipulates that God-Father creates through God-Son, the
creative Verbum,[58] so that the Verbum is the unique hypostasis of
rectitude. This 'uncreated rectitude' is the norm of all rectitudes: the reality and truth of (created) things arise from
their proximity to Him.[59]

In the Verbum, justice, truth and rectitude are identified.[60] He is the ultimate uncreated norm. The rectitude of
things consists in their fidelity to this Supreme Rectitude,
their 'existendi veritas.' In this fidelity they are what they
ought to be: "Supreme Truth, subsisting in and for itself, is
not the truth of any particular thing; but, when some thing is
in accordance with the Supreme Truth, then we speak of the truth
or rectitude of that thing."[61] Whatever is, insofar as it is,
is what it ought to be. This truth or rectitude of the existence
of things is both cause and effect as it is the cause of the rectitude of thought and propositions and the effect of Supreme Rectitude. However, the rectitude (or truth) of thought and proposition does not ground any other rectitude.[62] In De Veritate,
Anselm enumerates an imposing catalogue of 'rectitudes' or
'truths': of propositions, thought, will, actions, senses,
things. Most important are truth, defined as "rectitudo sola
menti perceptibilis," and justice, "rectitudo voluntatis propter
se servata."[63] Freedom is the necessary precondition for both
allowing the will to choose the good and the mind to know the
truth.[64] The proper exercise of reason and will is entails the
acquiescence of the individual to the very structure of ultimate
reality.

Due to original sin man was exiled from justice; he lost
rectitude of the will and suffered a 'twisting around' in which
he replaced God as his center. The body became subjected to

corruption and the animal appetites while the soul was infected
with carnal desire.[65] The Incarnation effects a restoration of
the _rectus ordo_ which was violated by original sin. It does so
by uniting justice and reason.[66] Faith restores the rectitude
of the will (justice) counteracting the centrifugal movement
initiated by original sin by a centripetal motion of return to
God. This return entails a correlation between the knowledge of
God, self-knowledge and spiritual perfection. This work of 'humana restauratio' is a favorite theme of Anselm's running through
both the _Epistola de Incarnatione Dei_ and the _Cur Deus Homo_.

     The important point is that even in his doctrine of original
sin, emphasis rests on the loss of justice not on the weakening
of reason. True enough, once justice is recovered through faith
then reason can, in fact should, seek ever more profound understanding but the point of departure for faith is still a reason
capable of understanding. Even the understanding proceeding from
faith cannot exhaust that reality adumbrated by faith.[67] This is
because of its overwhelming intelligibility, not because of any
irrational residue: they are still reasons whether or not human
understanding can uncover them.[68] Anselm's remarks of the _Cur
Deus Homo_ are typical: "however far human statement can go, the
more profound explanation of so great a subject remains still
hidden."[69] This does not mean that the believer is exempt from
the exigencies of living faith. Further advances in truth are
always possible as "it often happens that God makes clear what
was obscure before."[70]

                    The Status of Reason

     As the legitimacy of unredeemed reason has been upheld
against Barth, before returning to collect the loose ends it may
be well to say a few words regarding Anselm's notion of the goal
of rationality. Here, as in other matters, Anselm follows
Augustine, who cites Varro's lost _De Philosophia_, in which the
Roman lists no less than 288 'schools' which though they disa-
greed on many particulars, agreed unanimously that man's primary
concern was the attainment of good and the avoidance of evil.[71]
In the _De Trinitate_, Augustine subordinates knowledge (scientia)
to wisdom (sapientia), though, strictly speaking, wisdom is a
species of the genus knowledge, because wisdom is knowledge which
ensures happiness, guiding man to it as his final end.[72] Anselm
follows in this tradition. rationality was given to man "in
order to distinguish between right and wrong, between good and
evil, and between the greater good and the lesser good."[73] He
was created for the purpose of loving and choosing the Supreme
Good as an end in itself.[74] The "iucunditas immortalitatis" of
Proslogion I is man's ultimate aspiration.[75] To arrive at its

goal man must follow justice (rectitude observed for its own sake) and not be deceived by apparent well-being. In short, man must 'perform' the truth of his nature.[76] This can be summed up by a previously cited text:

> "I realize that the understanding we achieve in this life is a mean between faith and direct vision... the more anyone advances towards understanding, the closer he approaches the direct vision we all eagerly desire."[77]

The rectitude of the existence of things is the cause of rectitude of thought and is itself the effect of Supreme Rectitude: God, things, thought, in that order. In the _Proslogion_ argument the 'thing' involved as God Himself represented by the privileged description of 'aliquid-quo-nihil-maius-cogitari-possit.' Strictly speaking, there is no middle term involved as the argument goes straight from 'that-than-which-nothing-greater-can-be-thought' to the reality signified, God. The Fool's error consists in remaining on the level of mere words (vox) and not advancing to the level of the reality (res) signified. Although it is true that there is a development of the argument in the second and third chapters, the transition from mental to real existence in _Proslogion_ II seems to be an optical illusion necessary for its didactic unfolding. After all, the transition is really not from mental to real existence but rather from a temporal, contingent mode of existence to its primary instance and source, the ground of both cognitional and real existence. God qua necessary being does not arise until the third chapter. Anselm shows that the cognitional order contains a plus or excess which, when attentively considered, directs our attention to its transcendent root and ground.

In view of Anselm's insistence that God is Simple Eternity Itself, enjoying ubiquity, obviating the difference between inner and outer, mental and real, a case may be made that in the _Proslogion_ we are dealing with that rectitude of the proposition which Anselm calls its natural truth of signification.[78] This means that the accidental truth of signification, based on the correspondence of proposition and state-of-affairs is transcended since God is not a thing (in this sense) nor subject to limitations. Natural truth is characterized by intelligibility, and grounds the accidental truth. Sounds without meaning cannot affirm what the case is.[79] Because of this it will ultimately be intelligibility that acts both as the point of departure and moving force in the development of the argument. The Fool's understanding of 'something-than-which-nothing-greater-can-be-thought' initiates the demonstration proper, and each transition to a fuller and deeper understanding, (from mental to real existence (<u>Proslogion</u> II), to necessary existence (<u>Proslogion</u> III), to the realization that God is something greater than can be thought (<u>Proslogion</u> XV) takes place under the aegis of the principle of noncontradiction. The truth of the proposition, 'something-than-which-nothing-greater-can-be-thought exists' is not a question of correspondence with an external state of affairs as the terms necessary for correspondence (inner: outer) have been transcended.

In this chapter, we have attempted to present Anselm's notion of reason and faith in all its complexity, and have demonstrated that there is a legitimate exercise of reason without as well as within the domain of faith. The understanding that follows faith is unique in directing the knower to his ultimate end, the vision of God. Insofar as the Fool is concerned we have solved the riddle presented by his disappearance after <u>Proslogion</u> IV and the problem which he, as unbeliever, presents to the believer. Lastly, a few tentative remarks prepared the way for a continuation of our exposition in the next chapter in which necessary reasons and the problem of intellectual illumination will be considered, both of great importance to <u>Proslogion</u> interpretation.

NOTES

1. Epistola 129, Opera Omnia III, 271, 3-6.

2. Epistola 136, III, 280, 16-26.

3. Ibid., 280, 32-281, 38.

4. Ibid., 281, 38-41.

5. Op. cit., (Opera Omnia, II), 8, 7-19.

6. Ibid., 8, 19-9, 1.

7. Ibid., 7, 5-8, 1. In the 'correct order,' as noted in the Proslogion, faith takes precedence over understanding in accordance with Is. 7:9 "nisi credideritis, non intelligetis." Here Anselm follows, along with Augustine, the old Latin translation of the Septuagint. Anselm of Canterbury: Trinity, Incarnation, and Redemption, ed. and trans. J. Hopkins, and H. W. Richardson (New York: Harper and Row, 1970), p. 8, note 4.

8. Ibid., 9, 9-11.

9. "In multimodos errores per intellectus defectum cogantur descendere," Ibid., 7, 12-8, 1.

10. Ibid., 9, 20-10, 4.

11. Idem. Anselm may well have been influenced in his notion of 'dialectiae haeretici' by Augustine's view of intellectual 'cupiditas' found in the De Trinitate. As the mind wants everything for itself and the body is the only thing it can call its own, the mind feeds on the images and sense-forms, wallowing in them. It becomes subject to matter and turns away from the reality of the Ideas. De Trinitate XII, 8, 13; 10, 15; 12, 17.

12. Op. cit., 9, 21.

13. Ibid., 8, 20.

14. Ibid., 15, 33.

15. Ibid., 14, 31.

16. Ibid., 12, 27.

17. Dial., 4 cited by Kenneth E. Kirk, The Vision of God (New York: Harper and Row, 1966), p. 37ff.

18. Epistola de Incarnatione Verbi, IV, 17, 14-19.

19. Ibid., 18, 4-7.

20. Ibid., XIII, 31, 1-9; VII, 22, 1ff; 10ff.

21. Ibid., XV, 33, 12; 33, 28-34, 2ff.

22. Ibid., VI, 20, 16-19.

23. Ibid., 21, 1-4. Ibid., 20, 22-24.

24. Barth, op. cit., pp. 104-106.

25. Charlesworth, op. cit., p. 46.

26. Hayen, op. cit., p. 165; 169.

27. Opera Omnia II; De Concordia, III, (VI), 270, 23-25.

28. Ibid., 270, 28-30. Also, Ibid., 271, 5-9.

29. Ibid., 271, 8-9.

30. Ibid., 271, 15-19.

31. Ibid., 270, 28.

32. Proslogion, XIV, (Opera Omnia I), 111, 12-13.

33. By Charlesworth. op. cit., p. 30. He reflects the general consensus of opinion. Barth calls it technically perhaps Anselm's most complete work, op. cit., p. 36.

34. Loc. cit., (Opera Omnia II), 40, 10-12.

35. Ibid., 40, 1-2.

36. Ibid., 40, 4-5.

37. This is put by Anselm into the mouth of Boso. Ibid., I, 1, 48, 16-18.

38. This seems to be Barth's contention.

39. Op. cit., II, 22; 133, 3-11.

40. Ibid., I, 3; 50, 16-22.

41. Barth. op. cit., p. 18.

42. Epistola de Incarnatione Verbi (Opera Omnia II) I, 5, 10-13.

43. For the distinction between 'dead' and 'living' faith,
    Monologion LXXVIII, (Opera I), 84, 16-85, 9; Cur Deus Homo
    (Opera II), I, 1, 47, 8-11; Ibid., 48, 16-24.

44. Barth, op. cit., p. 21.

45. Ibid., p. 33.

46. Ibid., p. 37.

47. Ibid., pp. 64-65.

48. Ibid., p. 71.

49. Ibid., pp. 53-54.

50. Cur Deus Homo, II, 16, 117, 18-22; I, 2, 50, 3-13; et al.

51. Sigmund Freud, Introductory Lectures on Psychoanalysis,
    Standard Edition, Complete Psychological Works, Vol. XVI
    (London: The Hogarth Press, 1971), p. 436ff.

52. De Concordia, III, (VI), 272, 6-7.

53. "Spero per auxilium eiusdem sancti spiritus quia--si malunt
    solidae veritati acquiescere quam pro inani victoria
    contendere--per hoc quod absque ambiguitate confitentur, ad
    hoc quod non recipiunt, rationabiliter duci possunt........
    pro certissimis argumentis ad probandum quod non credunt utar"
    Op. cit., (Opera II), I, 177, 7-10; 16-17.

54. Ibid., XIII, 211, 24, 27.

55. Op. cit., (Opera II), VII, 232, 4-5.

56. Epistola de Incarnatione Verbi, VI, 20, 16-19. Cur Deus Homo,
    II, 22, 133, 5-9.

57. Robert Pouchet, O.S.B., La Rectitudo chez Saint Anselme (Par-
    is: Etudes Augustiniennes, 1964), p. 15. Dom Pouchet notes
    that the adjective rectus is used frequently in the Vulgate
    (in the psalms principally) and that it 'prendra une colora-

tion juridique et légaliste ou s'élargira en une conception sapientelle ou même religieuse," op. cit., pp. 30-31, especially Note #1. It should be noted that rectitude was first explicitly noted in De Veritate, written cir. 1080-1085, though implicitly present in Anselm's previous works.

58. Refer especially to chapters XXXII and XXXIII of the Monologion, 50, 15-53, 12.

59. De Veritate, (Opera Omnia I), XIII, 199, 27-29.

60. Ibid., XII, 192, 3-5; 6-10.

61. Ibid., XIII, 199, 27-29.

62. Ibid., X, 190, 7-12.

63. Ibid., XI, 191, 19-20; XII, 194, 26.

64. De Libertate Arbitrii (Opera Omnia I), III, 212, 13-18.

65. De Conceptu Virginali et de Originali Peccato (Opera Omnia II), II, 141, 9-15. Ibid., XV, 157, 3-8; also Ibid., XIX, 160, 3-4.

66. Cur Deus Homo, II, 1, 97, 14-18; IX, 61, 13-16.

67. Ibid., Commendatio, 40, 4-5. Also Ibid., I, 2, 50, 12-13; II, 16, 117, 18-22, et al.

68. Ibid., II, 16, 117, 18-22. For Anselm "Deus nihil sine ratione facit," Ibid., II, 10, 108, 23-24. Also Ibid., I, 8, 59, 10-11.

69. Ibid., I, 2, 50, 12-13.

70. Ibid., I, 1, 49, 3-6. Following the injunction of Matthew 10;8, "Freely have you received; freely give," it is possible to penetrate deeper into Truth. In Boso's words "reminisci quia saepe contingit in colloquendo de aliqua quaestione, ut deus aperiat quod prius latebat; et sperare de gratia dei quia, si ea quae gratis accepisti libenter impertiris, altiora ad quae nondum attigisti merreberis accipere." Idem.

71. De Civitate Dei, XIX, 1-2; XVIII, 39.

72. De Trinitate, XII, 12, 17; XII, 15, 25; XV, 1, 3. As Gilson rightly indicates, "This doctrine explains why Augustine during the Middle Ages will always oppose any effective distinction between philosophy and theology. To separate

science from wisdom would be to render both impossible."
<u>The Christian Philosophy of Saint Augustine</u> (New York: Random House, 1960), p. 304, note 22.   See also the same author's <u>La Philosophie de Saint Bonaventure</u>, Spanish translation by Zudaire (Buenos Aires: Dedebec, Ediciones Desclée de Brouwer, 1947), Chapter II.

73. <u>Cur Deus Homo</u>, II, 1, 97, 4-11.

74. <u>Ibid.</u>, 97, 14-15.

75. <u>Proslogion</u>, I, 99, 5.

76. Anselm speaks of 'doing' the truth and equates it with 'doing' good.   "Idem est veritatem facere quod est bene facere.. .... Unde sequitur quia rectitudinem facere est facere veritatem.   Constat namque facere veritatem esse bene facere, et bene facere esse rectitudinem facere.   Quare nihil apertius quam veritatem actionis esse rectitudinem." <u>De Veritate</u>, V, 181, 21-22; 25-28.

77. <u>Cur Deus Homo</u>, Commendatio, 40, 10-12.

78. Anselm speaks of two '<u>significationis veritate</u>,' the first, when a proposition affirms what is the case and denies what is not the case. (<u>De Veritate</u>, II 177, 10-12); the second, the meaning of the proposition, which remains the same whether that which the proposition asserts to be the case is or isn't the case. (<u>Ibid.</u>, 178, 1-4.) A proposition is 'correct and true' when (1) it signifies in accordance with its power of signifying, and (2) it signifies in accordance with the 'purpose' for which it has the power of signifying. (<u>Ibid.</u>, 179, 10-12);(<u>Ibid.</u>, 179, 19-25.)

79. <u>Ibid.</u>

CHAPTER IV

NECESSARY REASONS

At this juncture the question of necessary reasons should be broached. In most instances in which Anselm uses the term 'reason' he links it to the notion of necessity: to speak of reason is to speak of necessary reasons.[1] He explicitly states that the _Proslogion_ was written with the express purpose of demonstrating through necessary reasons. The peculiar nature of the _rationes necessariae_ which uncover the 'that' (_quia sunt_) while leaving the 'what' (_quomodo sint_) in obscurity, and which may be either strict, logically necessary demonstrations, or merely reasons for truths already known, should be determined. Anselm is, in part, to blame for their controversial status--the Jacquin-Ottaviano debate of the thirties has yet to be satisfactorily resolved[2]--as he does not use necessary reasons in one uniform manner but submits them to varied and at times, rather startling, metamorphoses.

Anselm invariably proceeds from that which is true and accepted as true not only to himself but also to his adversary, and proceeds to show the necessary character of the implications which follow from this common ground. This common ground acts as the point of departure for demonstration. His opponents cannot deny all the truths accepted by Anselm. Indeed, from his point of view, they cannot and still remain rational beings. They accept one or more which becomes the substructure from which logical consistency or inconsistency can be shown. Because of this, Anselm has a preference, as Southern correctly indicated, for proceeding by equipollent propositions rather than by syllogisms.[3] The _Proslogion_ is unique in that the only common ground between Anselm and the Fool, the believer and the unbeliever, is a shared humanity and reason. If this were not the case, if there existed no common ground between Anselm and the Fool, we would then be justified in adopting Barth's hypothesis that all discussion with the _insipiens_ is pointless.[4]

The use Anselm makes of necessary reasons indicates the distance which separates him from modern or contemporary philophical method. In the _Monologion_ and _Proslogion,_ he attempts to prove almost the whole deposit of Christian belief concerning God with the exception of the Incarnation.[5] In his effort to answer the opponents of Christianity and help the conscientious striving of the believer who humbly seeks to understand what is already believed,[6] Anselm is aware that he is innovating, and may be suspect to his ecclesiastical brethren. Referring back to these works from the vantage point of the _Epistola de Incarnatione_

Verbi he denies any attempt to correct the 'Catholic doctors,' but rather "to give expression to things about which, perchance, they were silent, but which yet are not out of harmony with their teaching."[7] His first work, the Monologion, advises those who would denounce him to read diligently St. Augustine's book on the Trinity, and then judge in its light.[8] Nothing has been stated which is inconsistent with the writings of the catholici patres.[9] Here, again, within the limits of belief, without any opponent to contend with, Anselm uses fides to extend intellectus. A good indication of the novelty of this method is the obvious disfavor with which Lanfranc, known to the age primarily as a dialectician,[10] received it. As far as we know, Anselm did not send the Archbishop any other work that he wrote during the next ten years.[11]

In the Cur Deus Homo, Anselm proposes to understand by 'rational necessity' that all those things which the Catholic faith requires us to believe regarding Christ must be true if we wish to be save.[12] The one article of belief that had been omitted from the program of both Monologion and Proslogion, the Incarnation, is here broached. From the basis that man was created to enjoy a blissful immortality, and that it is necessary for him to achieve the purpose of creation, Anselm goes on to 'prove' that this can occur only through a man-god.[13] Leaving Christ to one side, remoto Christo, as if nothing were known about him, Anselm proceeds with the demonstration.[14]

The De Grammatico opens with the statement that the problem under consideration--whether 'literate' (grammaticus) is a substance or a quality--is to be solved through necessary reasons.[15] In De Processione Spiritus Sancti, a justification of the Latin addition of the 'filioque' to the Creed, that the Holy Spirit proceeds from both the Father and the Son, he again speaks of desiring to lead the 'Greeks' rationally from that which they confess without hesitation to that which they do not as yet accept.[16] The Christian Orthodox belief, "the faith of the Greeks along with those things which they believe without any doubt," will provide the ground for the exercise of necessary reasons. The demonstration proceeds by means of 'certain arguments,' 'irrefutable arguments,' 'uncontestable arguments.'[17]

Anselm admits that this procedure is not really novel but has been used by both Latins and Greeks. To counter his opponent's insistence on the unscriptural basis of the filioque, Anselm points to Christian acceptance of the terms person or Trinity although they are not found in the prophets, evangelists, or apostles.[18] Nevertheless, they are deduced with meridional clarity from them just as is the filioque.[19]

Arguments of Fitness

As suggested previously there appears to be both a strict and a loose sense of necessary reasons. The problem is further complicated by Anselm's use of 'arguments of fitness (convenientia),' which are distinguished, albeit not too clearly, from necessary reasons. They should be accepted as 'beautiful pictures' which derive their strength from being painted on something solid, this solidity being the "rational soundness of truth, the necessity of inference."[20] Necessary reasons provide the ground for arguments of fitness. They are to be put on view like 'pictures' of the body.[21] By themselves, they may be attacked as fictions, as painting on a cloud, but linked to their ground of rational necessity, they serve to augment the beauty of truth.

But even this distinction between necessary reasons and arguments of fitness does not apply at all times. In the Cur Deus Homo, Anselm indicates that there was never a time since the creation of man in which at least one man was headed towards the goal he was created for. It would be incongruous that God should, for even a moment, permit the human race to exist without a purpose.[22] Boso, his companion in dialogue, immediately classifies this argument as a reason of fitness but adds that reasons of necessity can also be found for this conclusion.[23] However, instead of adducing these new reasons Boso proceeds to contrast Anselm's argument with its antithesis, concluding that "it is necessary that there was always someone who had a share in the reconciliation we have been discussing."[24] Further along, after demonstrating that it was necessary for divine and human natures to be united in one person, Anselm goes on to state that as it is more fitting that it occur in the person of the Word, it is necessary that God the Word and human nature be united in one persons.[25]

It appears that whenever a reason of fitness can be traced back to its source, or its antithesis demonstrated to be untenable, it then takes on the character of necessary reason. In any event, both the strict and loose varieties of necessary reason suffice to produce certitude. Reason is not exercised in a vacuum but rather deals with different things, and there is one 'thing'--Anselm often refers to God as a sort of super-substance--[26] which has its own unique exigencies. Insofar as God is concerned no reason however weak, is to be rejected, as in regard to Him, "whatever is unsuitable, however slightly, is consequently impossible" and "a rational argument, however weak, induces certainty, unless there is a stronger argument to refute it."[27] In the same vein, truth does not have to be be established by many arguments, a concatenation of necessary reasons. One argument will do. Whether demonstrated by one or many arguments truth is defended against doubt.[28] Anselm complicates matters by suggesting that certainty is subject to degrees. In the final passage of the first part of the _Cur Deus Homo_, Boso asks help in understanding by rational necessity those things which must be believed regarding Christ "et ut certiores sint argumentationes tuae, sic a longe incipe, ut eas super firmum fundamentum constituas."[29] Here again we encounter Anselm's method of anchoring his arguments on previously accepted truth. The more solidly they are anchored, the 'deeper' the reason, and the greater the certitude.

Perhaps this 'method' hinges on Anselm's recognition that divine reality is truly inexhaustible and ultimately opaque to human reason. Nevertheless it is possible to proceed by degrees, probing into more profound depths. The truths of faith are not irrational or arational but pertain to reasons, though it may occur that human reason because of its feebleness is unable to penetrate to the level of ultimate reasons. The will of God is never unreasonable and all things proceeding from him are intelligible though at times in a way that transcends human understanding.[30] Human reason can discover 'reasons' which were previously hidden and it often happens that God clarifies what was obscure.[31] There are always 'deeper reasons' and the process of discovery is unending.[32]

Necessity in this respect cannot be equated to absolute necessity since it is relative to and deduced from previously accepted truths. Although it produces conviction, it does not exhaust the reality under consideration, as it is open to further penetration by human reason. Barth was correct in believing that a progressive advance in knowledge is characteristic of Anselm's thought.[33] Because of this, necessary reasons are provisional as the discovery of 'deeper reasons' is always present. This may follow from Anselm's belief that absolute knowledge is reserved to God alone. Human knowledge is fragmentary and incomplete.[34]

Another important characteristic of necessary reasons is that while they can demonstrate the 'that,' the 'what' and the 'why' may remain unknown. In these cases the demonstration cannot be called into doubt, though we do not comprehend the 'reason' why it is so.[35] Whoever maintains that something which necessarily is, is impossible merely because he cannot comprehend why it is so, is a Fool, an insipiens.[36] The term 'Fool' arises not only in the Proslogion, but also in the Cur Deus Homo. The Monologion states that in the investigation of an uncomprehensible object it is enough to prove that it "most certainly exists" although the object itself remains opaque to reason and cannot be put into words.[37]

It is clear that neither necessary reasons nor arguments of
fitness consist of the unfolding of a given definition. They
are grounded on the 'data' which Christian faith has transmitted
and the human mind has meditated upon. It is the disproportion
between the truths of faith and the human mind which engenders
this type of argument. Chenu remarks that necessary reasons
develop human resonances which:

> "set off for the understanding both the nature of
> man and the mystery of his destiny, illuminating
> powers having more value than the surest geometrical
> patterns conceived by the mind."[38]

In contraposition to Anselm, who distinguishes between necessary
reasons, anchored on a previously given truth of faith,and reasons of fitness where this 'anchoring' has not been discovered,
later philosophers and theologians will tend to abolish the distinction altogether. Both become 'suitabilities,' what St.
Thomas called congruentes rationes, where "a reason is introduced,
not as furnishing a sufficient proof of a principle, but as con-
firming an already established principle, by showing the congru-
ity of its effects."[39]

Reviewing the preceding it is clear that necessary reasons
are not esoteric noetic fauna but rather deductions grounded on
previously accepted truth which are able to produce certitude.
Admittedly, this covers a multitude of sins and runs the gamut of
all senses of necessary reasons. There certainly is a difference
in the logical rigor used discussing necessity in the Cur Deus
Homo[40] and the necessary reasons used defending the filioque. It
does not seem that Anselm distinguished between them as both
suffice to produce certitude. The stronger the credal base the
looser the necessary reasons; the weaker the credal base the
stricter the necessary reasons.

The Proslogion and Necessary Reasons

The unique character of the Proslogion is manifested by the
difficulty in uncovering any credal base linking Anselm and the
Fool. The only common ground is a shared humanity and reason,
which, as has been previously noted, are operative aside from the
acceptance of belief. Because of this, the reasoning displayed
in the argument is most rigorous. It is only after God is found
to be 'quidquid melius est esse quam non esse' that the looser
form of argument makes an appearance, in which necessary reasons
and arguments of fitness tend to blend. As there is no common
credal base the encounter must take place on the field of reason.
Anselm must proceed by reason alone, ratio sola.

The description of God, 'aliquid quo maius nihil cogitari potest,' acts as the bridge between Anselm and the Fool. It is the point of departure for the Proslogion enterprise. If it is not understood, at least in part, the whole enterprise has to be aborted. Gaunilo was aware of this and directed his criticisms in this direction. To see in 'something-than-which-nothing-greater-can-be-thought' a peculiarly Christian 'proclamation' of the Name of God, as does Barth,[41] is rather speculative. Even Vignaux, who seems receptive to this view, admits that neither a scriptural nor a traditional divine name can be recognized.[42] A better case could be made for 'necessary existence' which Maimonides appears to have suggested as a meaning for the Tetragrammaton.[43] However the Proslogion II description is explicitly mentioned as arising from belief: et quidem credimus te esse aliquid quo nihil maius cogitari possit. In the texts cited by Father Schmitt, there are similar descriptions to be found in Augustine, Boethius, and others.[44]

Anselm himself, in the Monologion, considered a sort of De Trinitate in the Middle Ages, indicates that all who affirm God's existence, whether one or many (sive unum, sive plures), think of Him as that which is above every other nature.[45] Therefore it is not unique to Christian belief as even polytheists accept it, though to a Christian it would doubtless signify the triune God of his belief and provide the point of departure for the knowing and loving of God. To the unbeliever it provides the initial seed of meaning which may or may not issue in belief. Although the believer is grounding his understanding of the description of God on previously accepted faith, the Fool only 'knows' the description, and that of course only in a truncated manner. In the best of cases, it may lead the Fool to renounce his foolishness and to believe in God. After all, only the name 'God' is properly applicable to the Supreme Being.[46] Anselm is not really interested in discovering whether there is an absolutely incommunicable name that applies to God and to Him alone,[47] since His ineffability is safeguarded even if He has never been named according to the peculiar nature of His being.[48] Nonetheless, that Anselm's description is not peculiarly Christian does not mean that it is not in continuity with certain aspects of Christian tradition. God is described only in an indeterminate fashion and in a negative manner.[49]

Whether or not Anselm distinguished between strict and loose use of necessary reasons--we have good reason to think he did not --the Proslogion becomes a specifically philosophical task, in the post-Cartesian sense,[50] insofar as it is based on the former. It ceases to be one when the strict use ends and the argument proceeds along the less rigorous lines of fitness. The principle of contradiction provides the continuity which leads the argument from (1) mental to real existence, (2) real existence to necessary existence, and (3) necessary existence to ineffable existence. Its point of departure is the God-description and human reason. The description is, as indicated, unique, and the argument cannot be developed on other lines. This is why Anselm discards the name 'God' or the description 'greatest being.'[51] Another peculiarity of the Proslogion is that it is the intelligibility of 'that-than-which-nothing-greater-can-be-thought' which is really at stake, not its existential status. Anselm could hardly expect the Fool, who had denied the existence of God, to immediately affirm it.

There is a peculiar confusion which is endemic to Proslogion interpretation and is difficult to dispel. This accounts, at least in part, for the feeling that no matter how strongly the argument impresses itself on us, or how fallacious it may seem, mere affirmation or denial misses the mark. We are aware that something has eluded us. Much of this is due to the alien culture to which Anselm belonged and the intepreter's proclivity to impose categories which do not correspond to the exigencies of the argument. There is another reason. Anselm proceeds according to a movement which, in outline, may be described as: intelligibility-necessity-existence, not quite according to the chronological order of the argument as described above. The confusion lies in viewing Proslogion II as an argument in its own right not as a preliminary stage, its conclusion (that 'aliquid-quo-maius-nihil-cogitari-potest' exists 'in re') dependent on the subsequent chapter.

The Development of the Argument

In order to prove this and to follow the development of a chain of necessary reasons we must return to the beginning, to Anselm's description of God to the Fool, who understands what he hears. If it is understood at all it may be said to have conceptual existence (esse in intellectu). It is put on the level of both real things, which exist both in reality and in the mind, and imaginary or fictional entities, which exist only in the mind.

Once admitted that it does exist in intellectu, it must then be thought of as existing in reality. Otherwise, it could not be thought at all. The principle of contradiction is brought into play: Anselm is not comparing one 'god' with another 'god,' the "God existing in knowledge and in objectivity" to the "God existing only in knowledge."[52] Rather, he is stating that not to include existence within the notion of 'that-than-which-nothing-greater-can-be-thought' is contradictory and the outcome would be unintelligible: mere nonsense. If 'quo-maius-cogitari-non-

<u>potest</u>' is '<u>quo-maius-cogitari-potest</u>,' then it is nothing at all.
It is unintelligible. But as its intelligibility had previously
been admitted—the Fool understands what he hears—either real
existence is accepted or intelligibility itself is put in jeop-
ardy.

Further, if we are correct in assuming that the existence
Anselm has in mind, at this point of the argument, is what we
have called, with Barth, general existence; (that existence in
common with all existing things), existence <u>in re</u> as here affirmed is certainly not the unique, necessary, existence which is
proper to God, unless Anselm is looking over his shoulder from
the vantage-point of <u>Proslogion</u> III, already incorporating it in
his conclusion. Perhaps he is paralyzing the movement of the
argument for didactic purposes, giving the reader a point of
reference to aid his understanding, rendering his original insight
into discursive reason. At any rate, 'something-than-which-
nothing-greater-can-be-thought' is not identified as God until
the third chapter: "<u>Et hoc es tu, domine deus noster</u>."[53]

It is enough for the development of the argument to conclude
that 'something-than-which-nothing-greater-can-be-thought' must
at least be thought of as really existing. The next step is to
prove that it exists so truly, in such a unique manner, that it
cannot even be thought not to exist. Everything which does
exist, although it cannot be understood (<u>intelligere</u>) not to
exist, can be thought (<u>cogitare</u>) not to exist. Only 'something-
than-which-a-greater-cannot-be-thought' cannot even be thought,
'imagined,' not to exist. If the denial were effected a contradiction would ensue and it would entail the denial of intelligibility, an intelligibility previously admitted by the Fool.

Many comparisons come to mind, a square circle, a triangle
whose three angles do not equal two right angles, but these do
not seem to hit the mark. Anselm's description is unique in that
it signifies God in the most indeterminate manner and would van-
ish <u>en bloc</u> were it demonstrated to be self-contradictory. A
square circle is a contradiction but one knows what a square and
a circle are. A Euclidean triangle whose three angles do not
equal two right angles is a contradiction but one knows what an
angle is. A being 'than-which-nothing-greater-can-be-thought'
which is a being 'than-which-a-greater-can-be-thought' is a contradiction, pure and simple. It means nothing. It is unintelligible. It is this threat to intelligibility, brought to light by
the use of the principle of contradiction, which is the moving
force in the development of the argument.

Anselm's Presuppositions

It should be pointed out at this point that Anselm takes for granted (a) that existence in re is superior to existence merely in intellectu, and (b) that a being whose non-existence is unthinkable is superior to a being whose non-existence is thinkable. The first arises from Anselm's belief that a thing has more reality in itself than it does in thought, that the truth of the existence of things is the cause of the truth in thought. The second and more hazardous presupposition hinges on the superiority of necessary being to contingent being. The non-thinkability of non-existence reflects necessity within the noetic field.

God's necessity, then, reaches out to display itself in a representation encountered in human consciousness, the description, 'something-than-which-a-greater-cannot-be-thought.' This being cannot even be thought not to exist. Faith, searching for understanding (intelligere), finds its way through the domain of thinking (cogitare), and in search of reality it wends its way through possibility. Anselm appears to have found a 'cogitare' which is an 'intelligere,' the point at which the possible and the real meet, which is condensed in the description of God.

A necessary being, who is whatever it is better to be than not to be,[54] is limitless and eternal, enjoying existence "simul et ubique totum."[55] It has no beginning and no end. As Anselm stresses in the Responsio, whatever exists in the mind only and not in reality, can be thought of as having a beginning, and therefore its non-existence is thinkable.[56] Even if one has been considering existence in the mind alone, it follows that when 'something-than-which-a-greater-cannot-be-thought' is demonstrated to possess necessary existence, it transcends the mind/reality dichotomy. It must exist in an unique, privileged, manner, and not merely over against the mind. Gaunilo's 'lost island', for example, can be thought (imagined) not to exist. It is impossible to derive real existence from existence in the mind in these cases as even if the 'lost island' were to exist it would exist contingently. In Anselm's words:

> only that being in which there is neither beginning nor end nor conjunction or parts, and that thought does not discern save as a whole in every place and at every time, cannot be thought as not existing.[57]

The argument does not halt at this point but continues with the emphasis no longer on strict, rigorous, demonstration, but on meditations developed from the conclusion that God is "whatever it is better to be than not to be."[58] The fifteenth chapter is an exception. Anselm, again recurring to the principle of contradiction, proves that God is something greater than can be thought, "_maius quam cogitari possit_."[59] He is both known (as a necessary being) and unknown (in Himself). Anselm demonstrates the 'that' without touching the 'what' or the 'why.' But the proof is satisfactory, at least insofar as Anselm is concerned God has been found with "_tam certa veritate et vera certitudine_."[60] The argument now changes direction. The search for reasons--necessary reasons in the strict sense-- in the light of truth will become, after _Proslogion_ XV, a search for the light of truth itself.

This section has attempted to study Anselm's notion of necessary reasons and to trace their use in the _Proslogion_. It was ascertained that Anselm uses necessary reasons in both a strict and a loose sense, depending on the credal ground, the taken-for-granted truths, which a given argument uses as its point of departure. Anselm's reasons of fitness are grounded on necessary reasons and under certain circumstances, themselves acquire necessity.

The working out of the _Proslogion_ argument by necessary reasons in the strict sense was presented as following from the absence of credal ground, only reason uniting Anselm and the Fool. The use of the principle of contradiction, running intermittently from the second to the fifteenth chapter, from the conclusion that God exists in reality, to the conclusion that He is greater than can be thought, reflects this strict use of necessary reasons. An attempt was made to structure the argument, presented before in outline only, in such a way as to stress its cogency and rigor. This first and perhaps sketchy effort to make sense out of the properly philosophical sections of the _Proslogion_ will be supplemented by an analysis of the objections and reinterpretations which the argument has generated.

1. "Sed et si quis legere dignabitur duo parva mea opuscula, _Monologion_ scilicet et _Proslogion_, quae ad hoc maxime facta sunt, ut quod fide tenemus de divina natura et eius personis praeter incarnationem, necessariis rationibus sine scripturae auctoritate probari possit." _Epistola de Incarnatione Verbi_, 6 (_Opera_ II): 20, 16-19.

2. The interplay between faith and the exercise of necessary reasons was the main point of contention. While Jacquin indicated that the Scriptures provided both point of departure and norm for necessary reasons, Ottaviano upheld the autonomous nature of their exercise. Furthermore, while Ottaviano tended to view them as rigorous demonstrations, Jacquin interpreted them as arguments grounded on credal truth which are able to generate certitude. A. M. Jacquin, "Les _rationes necessariae_ de Saint Anselm," in _Mélanges Mandonnet_ (Paris: Vrin, 1930), II, pp. 67-78; C. Ottaviano, "Les _rationes necessariae_ de Saint Anselm," in _Sophia_, I (1933), pp. 92-97. Also refer to Sofia Vanni-Rovighi, _S. Anselmo e la filosofia del secolo XI_ (Milano: Fratelli Boca, 1949), p. 81ff.

3. _St. Anselm and his Biographer_, p. 23.

4. Barth, _op. cit._, p. 65.

5. _Epistola de Incarnatione Verbi_, _loc. cit._

6. _Epistola de Incarnatione Verbi_, 6, 20, 20-21.

7. _Idem._

8. _Monologion_, _prologus_ (_Opera_ I); 8, 8-14.

9. _Idem._

10. Lanfranc was the first theologian to distinctly describe the change in the eucharistic elements in terms of the Aristotelian categories of substance and accident. See Southern, _op. cit._, p. 16ff.

11. _Ibid._, p. 26.

12. _Cur Deus Homo_, I, 25 (_Opera_ II), 7-13.

13. Ibid., praefatio, 42, 11-13; also 42, 13-43, 3.

14. Ibid.

15. De Grammatico I (Opera I); 145, 3-9. Especially, "Ideo quia
    videtur utrumque posse probari necessariis rationibus elle
    scilicet et non esse." (8-9). In translating 'grammatico'
    as 'literate' I am following D. P. Henry, The De Grammatico
    of St. Anselm (Notre Dame: University of Notre Dame Press,
    1964), No. 4, 107ff.

16. De Processione Spiritus Sancti, I (Opera II); 177, 14-17.

17. "certissimis argumentis," Idem.; "irrefragabilis rationes,"
    183, 15; "inexpugnabili ratione," 212, 11.

18. Ibid., XI; 209, 9-16.

19. Here, Anselm indicates that those who formulated the Creed
    did not want Christians to confess and believe only those
    things that were laid down. The 'Latins' have not corrupted
    the Creed, but only added something new--"sed aliud novum
    edidisse." Refer to Ibid., XIII; 211, 11-30.

20. Cur Deus Homo, I, 4 (Opera II); 51, 16-52, 6.

21. Idem.

22. Ibid., II, 16; 119, 3-10.

23. Ibid., 119, 13-18.

24. Idem.

25. Ibid., II, 9; 105, 12-106, 4.

26. The best discussion of the unique manner in which God can be
    said to be a substance is found in chapters 26-28 of the
    Monologion (Opera I); 44, 6-46, 31.

27. Cur Deus Homo, I, 10; 67, 1-6.

28. Ibid., I, 24; 94, 19-22.

29. Ibid., I, 25; 96, 6-15.

30. Anselm states, "Speciosa ratione super intellectu hominum,"
    Ibid., I, 1; 49, 19; also I, 20; 86, 21-22; and "Sufficere
    nobis debet ad rationem voluntas dei cum aliquid facit, licet
    non videamus cur velit. Voluntas namque dei numquam est

irrationabilis." <u>Ibid.</u>, I, 8; 59 10-11.

31. <u>Ibid.</u>, I, 1; 49, 3-6.

32. <u>Ibid.</u>, II, 16; 117, 18-22.

33. <u>Op</u>. <u>cit</u>., p. 32.

34. An interesting and subtle discussion of this point is given in <u>De</u> <u>Casu</u> <u>Diaboli</u>, 21; (<u>Opera</u> I), 266, 15-269, 8.

35. "A.Quid respondendum est illi, qui idcirco astruit esse impossibile quod necesse est esse, quia nescit quomodo sit? B. Quia insipiens est." <u>Cur</u> <u>Deus</u> <u>Homo</u>, I, 25; 95, 18-20. And "Quod enim necessaria ratione veraciter esse colligitur, id in nullam deduci debet dubitationem, etiam si ratio quomodo sit non percipitur." <u>Ibid.</u>, 96, 2-3.

36. <u>Idem</u>.

37. "Qua propter si ea quae de summa essentia hactenus disputata sunt, necessariis sunt rationibus asserta: quamvis sic intellectu penetrari non possint, ut et verbis valeant explicari, nullatenus tamen certitudinis eorum nutat soliditas." <u>Monologion</u>, 64; 75, 7-10. Also refer to preceding text, 74, 30-75, 6.

38. See M. D. Chenu, <u>Introduction</u> <u>a</u> <u>l'étude</u> <u>de</u> <u>Saint</u> <u>Thomas</u> <u>d'Aquin</u> (Paris: Vrin, 1950), translated by A. M. Landry and D. Hughes, <u>Toward</u> <u>Understanding</u> <u>Saint</u> <u>Thomas</u> (Chicago: Henry Regnery Co., 1964), see "The Procedures of Construction," pp. 156-199, esp. pp. 181-186.

39. "....inducitur ratio, non quae sufficienter probet radicem, sed quae radici iam positae ostendat congruere consequentes effectus." <u>Summa</u> <u>Theologiae</u>, 1a. pars, q. 32, 2.1, ad 2.

40. <u>Op</u>. <u>cit</u>.,II, 17, especially, 125, 8-25.

41. <u>Op</u>. <u>cit</u>., pp. 113ff, 122.

42. Paul Vignaux, <u>Philosophie</u> <u>au</u> <u>moyen</u> <u>âge</u>, trans. by E. C. Hall, <u>Philosophy</u> <u>in</u> <u>the</u> <u>Middle</u> <u>Ages</u> (Cleveland: Meridian, 1959), pp. 42-43.

43. Armand, C. Mauer, "St. Thomas on the Sacred Name 'Tetragrammation," in <u>Medieval</u> <u>Studies</u>, (Vol. XXXIV), 1972, p. 283ff.

44. <u>Opera</u> I, p. 102. There a possibility that Anselm adapted the description from Seneca. It is known that two copies of

Seneca's Quaestiones Naturales existed at Bec in the Twelfth century, in the preface of which the description of God as 'that-than-which-nothing-greater-can-be-thought' is found. G. Becker, Catalogi Bibliothecarum Antiqui, p. 202, No. 104; p. 266, no. 136, cited by Southern, op. cit., p. 59. Southern seems to think that Seneca was only speaking of physical magnitude (Id.).

45. Monologion, 80; 86, 19-21.

46. Ibid., 86, 17-18.

47. The speculations on the Tetragrammaton seem to have been alien to Anselm's thought, although some information was available by way of Saint Jerome, Alcuin and the Venerable Bede. It is interesting to note that Aquinas also seems to have overlooked these sources and to have recurred principally to Maimonides. See: Armand Mauer, op. cit., pp.275-286. Especially pp. 281-283.

48. The medium of access of God is through creatures, especially the human mind: "Patet itaque quia sicut sola est mens rationalis inter omnes creaturas, quae ad eius investigationem assurgere valeat, ita nihilominus eadem sola est, per quam maxime ipsamet ad eiusdem inventionem proficere queat." Monologion, 66; 77, 17-20.

49. Refer to Mauer, op. cit., pp. 275-278.

50. Descartes is here taken to represent the final breakdown of the Medieval view in which, to a greater (Augustinianism) or a lesser (Aristotelianism excluding the Averroists) extent scientia was viewed as directed to sapientia and subject to its exigencies.

51. Responsio, VII (Opera I); 136, 30-137, 1.

52. Barth, op. cit., p. 125.

53. Proslogion III; 103, 3.

54. Proslogion V; 104, 15-16.

55. Ibid., XIII; 110, 22; refer to the entire chapter, 110, 12-111, 5.

56. "Quidquid autem potest cogitari esse et non est, per initium potest cogitari esse." Responsio I; 131, 3-4. Also refer to I, 130, 20-132, 9 and IV; 133, 29-134, 6.

57. _Ibid._, IV; 134, 4-6.

58. _Proslogion_ V; 104, 15-16.

59. _Ibid._, XV; 112, 14-18.

60. _Ibid._, XIV; 111, 11-13.

CHAPTER V

THE PROSLOGION AS GNOSIS

"Le Proslogion n'est donc, autant que nous sachions, ni un traité de philosophie ni un traité de theologie, ni une contemplation mystique."[1] This evaluation of the Proslogion, given by Gilson some decades ago, still rings true as a reflection of the perplexity which the argument has been and is generating. Not unlike others, he is troubled by the apparent inconsistency between Anselm's method, which is purely rational and his object which transcends reason.[2] Gilson concludes that this unique form can be compared only with Christian gnosticism in the manner of St. Clement of Alexandria.[3] Centering his argument on Anselm's use of the word contemplatio, he rejects Dom Anselm Stolz' contention that the Proslogion is a piece of mystical theology.[4]

In fact, Anselm uses the term contemplatio only a few times, its meaning ranging from the purely religious—in a prayer he speaks of aeterna contemplatio gloriae Iesu—[5] to the strictly intellectual. Referring to the 'heretics of dialectic',he describes them as men whose minds are so covered over by corporeal images that they are unable to extract those things which should be contemplated purely by themselves.[6] The Cur Deus Homo was written explicitly not to attain to faith by way of reason, but to delight in the understanding and contemplation of what is already believed.[7] The Proslogion itself, as has already been noted is written "sub persona conantis erigere mentem suam ad contemplandum deum et quaerentis intelligere quod credit.[8] A further reference is found in a letter to the canon of St. Quentin (Gunther) who hesitated in accepting the office of Abbot. Anselm advises him to obey the demands of charity. Instead of living the life of sola contemplatio, Gunther should accept the dignity, while keeping in his heart the love of contemplation.[9] Finally, in another letter, Anselm stresses the importance of encouraging seculars to long for heaven and describes the Proslogion as the treatise in which he treated "de plenitudine beatudinis aeternae."[10]

Theoria and Contemplatio

These texts do not present a uniform character. Where one text justifies a spiritual interpretation, close to the litera-

ture of mysticism, others point to a cognitive philosophical
contemplation, close if not identical to the theoria of ancient
philosophy. That contemplatio was the Roman translation for
theoria further complicates matters, especially as the term had
suffered a metamorphosis since its use by the Hellenic philosophers. Theoria, in Aristotle, signifies a unique attitude towards the world in which truth and only truth is aimed at, a
directedness towards reality characterized solely by the desire
that the world will show itself to be such as it is in reality.[11]
It is the free discipline par excellence, fruit of leisure, simply good for nothing as it has no practical use. It is, in the
strictest sense, the science of truth.[12] Over sixteen centuries
later, Thomas Aquinas will reiterate this dictum though in a
form proper to his age: "philosophia prima non est practica, sed
specultativa, aequetur quod recte debeat dici scientia veri-
tatis."[13]

But whatever continuity exists between Aristotle and Aquinas
does not hold for the early Middle Ages in which the works of
Aristotle were almost unknown, except for the logica vetus
transmitted mainly through Boethius. At this time, as Dom Jean
Leclercq has indicated, the word theoria is often accompanied by
adjectives which indicate that it is now understood as a participation or anticipation of celestial contemplation, the vision of
God: theoria caelestis, theoria divina.[14] In these Benedictine
centuries, theoriae studia did not usually signify theoretical
studies but rather love of prayer. The archetype of the philosopher is no less than Christ Himself: "ipsa philosophia Chris-
tus."[15] In monastic literature, well into the twelfth century,
the expression christiana philosophia very often stands for the
monastic life.[16]

The two undoubted sources which could have moulded Anselm's
notion of contemplatio are Augustine and Gregory the Great. In
the De Trinitate, the contemplation of God 'face to face' is
promised as the end of our actions and the perfection of our joys,
as a joy that will never be taken from us.[17] In another work,
Augustine states explicitly that contemplation begins in this
life and is perfected in the next.[18] Augustine applies contemplatio to a wide spectrum of phenomena, from the operations of
the speculative intellect to the adumbration of the beatific vision.

Gregory's notion of contemplatio is more strictly spiritual,
the"raptim, per transitum" in which heaven 'opens' and a faint
glimpse of eternity is enjoyed. This is a moment of delight in
God, a wisdom that already flavors its object, "sapor, non sati-
etas." Contemplation is a knowledge through love to which all
men tend but which only the elect experience to its fullest, a
rapture in which the soul is raised beyond itself.[19]

This transformation of Hellenic _theoria_ into Christian _con-templatio_ is sometimes viewed as a fortuitous conjunction: the Platonic-Aristotelian notion of _theoria_ is supplemented by Christian _contemplatio_ which completes the act of philosophizing.[20] But this interpretation, possible only to hindsight, appears to minimize that basic antagonism between Greek philosophy and Christianity reflected in Paul's warning the Colossians,[21] Jerome's dream,[22] and Tertullian's fulminations.[23] Of course, a parallel, if not equally autochthonous, current may be appealed to: Justin Martyr and the Alexandrians. Nevertheless, the prevalence of warnings against _curiositas_, (a centering of attention on whatever is not God or in the service of salvation), is commonplace in the early Middle Ages and found in many texts of Augustine.[24] It is simply taken for granted that certain sacred things --say the Eucharist -- should not be calmly scrutinized but rather viewed with '_stupor et admiratio_.' In Anselm's lifetime, Alexander of Jumieges writes a treatise entitled _De Praescientia Dei, contra curiosos_.[25]

It is interesting to note that interest in _curiositas_ has surfaced in contemporary philosophy. Pieper indicates that it is the degeneration of the desire to 'see' and is a type of intemperance,[26] while Heidegger notes that this 'seeing' does not strive after the attainment of knowledge but rather after the possibilities of surrendering oneself to the world.[27] Today, _curiositas_ has generated a means of gratification which is always available and must be disciplined by temperance, an "asceticism of cognition" --the phrase is Pieper's--[28] to assure both a worthy human life and a true 'seeing' of reality.

Where does Anselm stand? Aimé Forest once indicated that the historian's greatest difficulty in regard to Anselm is to determine the proper function of speculation in the religious life.[29] This difficulty is reflected in the evident disaffection with which Dom Jean Leclercq, a discerning Anselm scholar from the viewpoint of spirituality, views his use of "the work of the intellect"; his "slightly ingenuous, possibly exaggerated, confidence in reason."[30] In this interpretation, Anselm's confidence in reason is disappointed and this disappointment turns him to fervent prayer.[31]

Experience

It may be advantageous to rephrase Forest's question, not asking about the proper function of speculation in the religious life but rather about the proper function of the religious life within speculation. This modification is justified for many reasons, not the least important of which are texts, of which the

Proslogion is one,which point to the fact that Anselm is seeking, as the goal of speculation, an experience of God:'*experiri*,' '*experientia*,' '*experimentum*' recur.[32] A rather obscure text of the *Epistola de Incarnatione Verbi* suggests that experience may lead to a knowledge higher than that which is obtained through hearing.[33] But instead of stopping at all ports of call let us return to the *Proslogion* text in the light of Anselm's conception of reason.

There is one important particular which, though previously mentioned in passing, should be noted here: the practical orien- tation of Anselm's thought. In his first work, the *Monologion*, Anselm insists that reason 'exists' for the purpose of judging what is good and what is evil and choosing the former. Reason is primarily displayed in judgment, judgment of degree of goodness. In accordance with the degree of goodness which a thing possesses it should be loved. Moreover, reason would be superfluous unless man loves that which it judges to be good and condemnes that judged to be evil.[34] God gives rational being to 'nothing' and constitutes it as a 'loving soul,' so that ultimately it may en- joy God Himself.[35] Whatever comprises man is directed towards his final goal. It is not without significance that the *Proslo- gion* ends with a meditation on the joy of the blessed.

For Anselm, as for Augustine, knowledge is directed to its completion in wisdom which is itself directed towards ultimate vision. Because of this,reason can be considered either from the perspective of its own work, autonomously, or from that of its function within the *fides-intellectus-visio* schema. From the first perspective, the goal of thought is to arrive at truth, rectitude perceptible by the mind alone. From the second, a grasping of truth which remains sterile, imprisoned within the cognitive order without generating love, is useless. From the perspective of man's ultimate end, reason is that function by which man comes to love God, present to his memory. In his use of memory, reason, and will to consider 'that which is above all else,' the rational creature fulfills its vocation to express, through voluntary imitation, the divine image which dwells within.

The fruition of God is the purpose of creation and present love gropes towards the beatific vision.[36] Reason is pointed towards love which it itself directed towards vision. They are not discrete strata but integral moments of a single process. Augustine's influence is again very much in evidence. The dis- tinction between *uti* and *frui* is certainly pertinent: to 'use' something is to take it as a means towards an end, while to 'en- joy' something is to affirm it on its own merits alone.[37] Strictly speaking, only God can be enjoyed i.e. affirmed on His own merits. To give a creature this divine prerogative, is to pervert the _raison d'être_ of creation and to fall into idolatry.

The privileged status of the human mind (_mens_) is clearly reflected in the _Proslogion_, that inner chamber of the soul where the image of God dwells, and where it is able to remember, think, and love God.[38] In the _Monologion_, the unique importance of the rational soul is spelled out in detail, repeating, extending, and adding precision to Augustinian themes. The _mens rationalis_ is that which most resembles God. Though every being, insofar as it exists, has some likeness to Him, the rational soul alone is capable of rising to the investigation of the Supreme Being.[39] As it is through the mind that God is approached, the more it discovers about its own nature the higher it rises in the knowledge of God.[40] In its ability to know, remember, and love itself, the mind is an image of the Trinity. In its ability to remember, know, and love God, the truer an image it becomes. This activity is equated by Anselm with wisdom itself.[41] The rational creature should devote all of his energies to the end for which he was created.[42]

As Gilson indicates, thinking is directed to a transcendent object in a purely rational way. But this is not an unsettling paradox. It is the logical outcome of a peculiarly unitary view of the human mind and its relation to ultimate reality, which Gilson, as a follower of St. Thomas, can hardly accept. Anselm continues classical _theoria_ in the importance given to the activity of thought, but provides it with a _practical_ orientation. He approaches the 'spiritual' sense of _contemplatio_ by making the vision of God the ultimate goal of life and thought but stops short of mystical contemplation in the strict sense. Whether or not these preliminary observations are accepted will be determined by a review of the _Proslogion_ text.

The Apophatic Aspect

Of special importance are chapters XIV-XXVI, where one encounters, in the words of Evdokimov, the _Proslogion's_ apophatic aspect.[43] The hermeneutic importance of _Proslogion_ XIV has only recently been noted by de Lubac.[44] Anselm having found and understood God, "_tam certa veritate et vera certitudine_"[45] returns to a theme of _Proslogion_ I. Although man is created to see God, he has not.God has been found, true enough, but solely on the level of intellect and this is not a 'seeing': "_Cur non te sentit, domine deus, anima mea, si invenit te._"[46] A true 'seeing,' a real encounter with God, is not limited to demonstration through necessary reasons, but must include experience, the experience of joy, the "_gaudium quoddam plenum, et plus quam plenum_"[47] of the blessed.

75

Reason is primarily the capacity for moral discernment, a discernment ultimately directed towards the possession and enjoyment of God. Knowledge is always knowledge of good and evil, the propedeutic to love, itself manifested through joy. Because of this knowledge which is restricted to the sphere of intellect would be a truncated thing and militate against the very purpose of creation which is to create rational, just, happy natures, destined to enjoy God.[48]

Proslogion XIV is then an affirmation that the argument has not been terminated, that the proof found in the second through fourth chapters, though satisfactory from the viewpoint of reason, still leaves something to be desired. There is an element yet to be incorporated and this element is experience: "to experience you."[49] This theme runs through chapters XVI, XVII and XVIII and even further as joy emerges as that privileged experience to which the believer gravitates through his rational activity. If particular goods are enjoyable, asks Anselm, how enjoyable is that good which contains the joyfulness of all goods? This is completely unique, "et non qualem in rebus creatis sumus experti, sed tanto differentem quanto differet creator a creatura."[50] Proslogion XXV is an almost rhapsodic tribute to the joy of the 'filii dei' in whom the love of God generates such immense joy that "tota anima non sufficiat plenitudini gaudii."[51] Knowledge, and love of God will grow 'here' and be made complete 'there', joy will be great in hope 'here,' and be complete 'there.'[52] The life of vision is not radically severed from the present life, but rather is its goal and completion. Growth in knowledge and love constitutes the bridge which connects the present life with the future life, this 'exsilium' to that 'patria.'

The Light Metaphor

A further theme initiated by Proslogion XIV is the distinction between the domain of light and truth, and the Light-Truth itself. From the "light of the understanding", Anselm moves to that light which is the source of all truth, "illa veritas, in qua est omne quod verum est, et extra quam non nisi nihil et falsum est."[53] The argument is displaced from the domain of cognition, as reflected in Proslogion II-IV to the Truth itself. If spatial metaphor were adequate, one could say that the movement of the Proslogion changes from the horizontal to the vertical, reminiscent of the ascent from diánioa to noesis in the analogy of the divided line of Republic (VI). The universe of discourse is different. One is no longer dealing with the laborious process of discernment and moral purification through which the 'lover of appearances' rises to the contemplation of reality and its source, propelled by eros, confident of the capabilities

of human nature. Here, the mystery of grace prevails, and dialectic is gradually transformed into prayer seeking contemplation. The action is primarily on the part of God not of man.

In the first chapter, Anselm refers to the inaccessible
light in which God dwells.[54] Proslogion XVI equates this "lux
summa et inacessibilis" with "tota et beata veritas."[55] Although
this 'light' overwhelms the intellect, whatever the mind 'sees',
it sees through this light.[56] The paradoxical still pursues
Anselm. Although closer to God, through understanding generated
by faith, he is still far from Him because of the lack of experience.[57] The 'senses' of the soul have become 'hardened,'
'dulled,' 'obstructed,' because of the "vetusto languore peccati."[58] The eighteenth chapter, although it begins on a less
than optimistic note--"conabar assurgere ad lucem dei, et recidi
in tenebras meas"[59] --uses the customary rhetorical and scriptural turns to implore God to ensure the ascent in progressive
knowledge, joy, and happiness.[60]

In his Responsio, Anselm again refers to the light metaphor,
this time relating it to the description of God as 'that-than-
which-a-greater-cannot-be-thought.' He agrees with Gaunilo's
opinion that it cannot be fully understood but adds that it would
be mistaken to conclude that it cannot be understood to any extent whatsoever: "then you must say that one who cannot see the
purest light of the sun directly does not see daylight, which is
the same thing as the light of the sun."[61] The description of
God can be understood in part in as much as certain of its properties are understood, such as that it refers to a necessary
being, not composed of parts, existing as a whole at every time
and in every place: "certe vel hactenus intelligitur et est in
intellectu 'quo maius cogitari nequit,' ut haec de eo intelli-
gantur."[62] The Johanine origin of the light-metaphor is betrayed
by the first lines of the section of De Veritate regarding the
truth of natural actions. God states that "qui male agit, odit
lucem" and "qui facit veritatem, venit ad lucem." It follows
that there is truth in actions.[63] Anselm is emphasizing the
ubiquity of rectitudo. Even actions are subsumed under it in
such a way that they can be described as 'doing' the truth.

This 'doing' includes not only actions but 'doing' the
truth, and 'doing' good.[64] Whosoever, then, abides in rectitude
comes to the light.[65] The necessary precondition for this ascent
appears to be the fidelity of all human activity to rectitude.
This straightens the 'curvature' caused by original sin and
points man to his ultimate goal. Rigorous thinking, the expansion of 'fides' into 'intellectus,' forms an integral moment of
this process.

As we have seen, five chapters, beginning with Proslogion

XIV, emphasize the difficulty of thinking about God and the futility of any pretension to exhaustive knowledge. However, Anselm goes on to speculate about God _qua_ Supreme Good, the Trinity, the state of the blessed, and his hopes for the possession of overflowing joy in the after life. From reasoning by means of 'light,' Anselm now approaches the 'light' itself. This process is truly praying in thought and for this reason, if none other, Gilson's characterization of the Proslogion as "gnosticisme chrétien," comparable with the doctrine of Clement of Alexandria, retains its value.

Gnosis: Anselm and Clement

Nonetheless, this comparison should not be abused. Great similarities between Anselm's _Proslogion_ and Clement's doctrine do exist: the intertwining of speculation and prayer, understanding as a spiritual exigency, contemplation as the goal of speculation, the stress on reason to the point of being considered suspect by less intellectual brethren.[66] But differences also exist, perhaps the principal issuing from the difference in cultural and spiritual milieu. Clement seems to equate reason with Greek philosophy, not an outrageous notion. But it does embarrass him as it has to be incorporated, it appears somewhat arbitrarily, into a hierarchy of which the _gnosis_ is Christ is the highest level.[67] In Anselm, reason is easily assimilated into the ascent to God. As stated above, faith is expanded into understanding, understanding generates love, and love strives for the possession and fruition of God.

There are other features of Anselm's approach which deserve mention. First of all, the emphasis he places on the continuity between present and future life. This is a restatement of his belief that understanding is the mean between faith and vision, that the more a person advances in understanding the closer he approaches vision.[68] The _Proslogion_ reflects this intimate relation between reason and spirituality, thought and prayer. The movement of reason towards God, taking place under the aegis of faith, is itself a sort of prayer as it gives witness to the truth. Thought and prayer are not separate activities but form part of the one movement towards the possession and fruition of God.

Leclercq misses the mark when he faults Anselm with a slightly ingenuous, possibly exaggerated, confidence in reason and considers him a disgruntled rationalist forced to turn to prayer. On the contrary prayer and rational argument do not meet in the _Proslogion_ as contending forces each struggling to supplant the other, but form integral parts of one process. Faith gives reason 'spiritual wings' and overcomes the temptation to institute a spiritually barren,self-satisfied science.[69] The more a thing is known as good the more is it loved. Therefore, reasoning about God has the same goal as prayer, to incite man to love God.[70] Prayer is not a placebo for a disappointed rationalist, but rather the natural outgrowth of rigorous thinking by means of necessary reasons.

The second feature which merits attention is that the unique joy discovered by Anselm, "gaudium plenum, et plus quam plenum,"[71] is not experienced in this life, though it is great in hope. Only in the other life will this joy be complete:"et ibi sit in re plenum."[72] From the perspective of spiritual life;the Proslogion argument obviously cannot be verified in this life it could take place only in the future life. This rules out a 'mystical' interpretation of the argument, such as that given by Dom Anselme Stolz.[73] It is not a piece of mystical theology. Although Dom Anselme is right in emphasizing the spiritual nature of the argument--the passage from faith to vision--[74] still, this transition hardly takes place in the pages of the Proslogion but is suggested as a future possibility and the object of the theological virtue of hope. Don Anselme's rather one-sided approach may be responsible for his failure in appreciating the importance of reason within the argument. Although he admits that Anselm has the intention of carrying out "theological speculative work,"[75] he neglects to inform us as to its specific nature.

The last chapters of the Proslogion emphasize the notion of God as Supreme Good, the root and ground of all being.[76] The fifth chapter already speaks of God as the Supreme Good which must contain "quidquid melius est esse quam non esse"[77] a Good which is incomprehensible.[78] God as Supreme Good is pressed in both the Monologion and De Conceptu Virginali.[79] Wycliff's notion, previously mentioned, that the argument is based on the convertibility of being and goodness (as God is 'summe ens' He is also 'summe Bonum'), should be noted at this point. Being dominates the first section of the Proslogion, the good is emphasized after the fifth chapter; 'something-than-which-nothing-greater-can-be-thought' is attributed existence in re (Proslogion II), necessary existence (Proslogion III), then identified with the Summum Bonum, which comprises 'whatever-it-is-better-to-be-than-not-to-be' (Proslogion V). Proslogion XXII identifies this being existing in a strict and absolute sense as the one and Supreme Good.[80] The final chapters speculate upon the nature of this Good and the character of the fruition which its possession ensures. The sadness and frustration of the first chapter is transformed into the expectation of the 'gaudium domini,' and the intellectual and spiritual exigencies of the Preface are satisfied.

The <u>Proslogion</u> was intended both as a meditation for the believer and a proof for the unbeliever. This is a valuable commonplace of Anselmian scholarship.[81] The very nature of <u>meditatio</u>, a hybrid form in which prayer and speculation merge, which Anselm was instrumental in shaping, reflects his originality. The term <u>meditatio</u> occurs very rarely in the Benedictine rule and refers to monastic activities such as learning the Psalter and preparing the lessons for the Office.[82] Under the influence of Anselm, <u>meditatio</u> suffers a metamorphosis and Chenu can speak of meditation as a strictly personal assimilative process which tends towards a grasp of the deeper nature of things.[83] In the twelfth century, Hugh of St. Victor speak of <u>meditatio</u> in terms of rejoicing:

> "to run freely in an open space where it (the
> mind) can fix its gaze on the truth without
> hindrance and investigate now this, now that,
> problem, until nothing is left doubtful or
> obscure."[84]

As a speculative form, meditation will fail to conform to the exigencies of the procrustean bed provided by the <u>Summae</u> and finally pass out of existence. It reflects the gradual disappearance of monastic culture as a theoretical force under the increasing pressure of the scholastic culture which reaches its apogee in the thirteenth century. The quasi-geometrical structure of the <u>Summae</u> is resistant to the literary style and experience oriented form of the meditation. Demonstration will rid itself of apiritually which will then be retired to the province of mystical theology.

But the <u>Proslogion</u> is much more than a speculative form. Hegel viewed the 'ontological argument' not merely as a proof justified by the <u>Logic</u> but the description of thought as the concrete march towards God, which justifies the <u>Logic</u>; "Hegel's <u>Logic</u> depends for its validity on the validity of the ontological proof."[85] It would be difficult to quarrel with "thought as the concrete march towards God" as an acceptable description of the argument. But it must be inserted within Anselmian context. The drift of the present chapter goes in a similar direction, the argument as the ultimate noetic consequence of thought about God.

Once we have come this far and look back to consider our previous observations, we encounter conclusions which may cause us disquiet. If thinking rigorously about God is an approach of

the whole man to God, a thinking about God lacking this goal
would be a mere _simulacrum_ limited to an order in which it remains unfruitful, in open contradiction to its own purpose and
function. Thought in regard to God which is not a sort of prayer, is not true thought. Thinking has an eminently practical nature; it generates love and leads to the fruition of the loved
object. _Theoria_ is not abolished but placed within the moral
order.

To view the _Proslogion_ as a _gnosis_ may well raise serious
objections but it is only by doing so that the fullness and dignity of the argument can be duly appreciated. Not to do so
would reduce it to a caricature of itself and frustrate the purpose of this introduction which is to present a serious interpretation of the argument. This should not minimize its philosophical aspect but merely suggests that even this aspect may be
evaluated within a wider context. Demonstration knows nothing of
eschatological verification, but if the argument does reach out
towards ultimate vision, it can only do so by way of truth. This
is why it is of the greatest importance to survey some of the
main philosophical objections to the argument which have been
presented in the course of about eight hundred years. In this
way, our position will be refined and clarified and the very possibility of the argument as _gnosis_ will be weighed, as far as
possible, on the scales of reason.

NOTES

1. Étienne Gilson, "Sens et Nature de L'argument de Saint Anselme" in _Arch. d'hist. et lit. du Moyen Age_ IX (1934),p.43.

2. _Ibid._, p. 47.

3. _Ibid._, p. 51.

4. "Jamais, à ma connaissance, it n'a désigné la contemplation de Dieu, telle que la decrit le _Proslogion_, comme une expérience de Dieu, et je n'arrive pas à trouver, dans tous les textes cités par le P. Stolz à l'appui de sa thèse, une seule formule où le mot sait employé par Saint Anselme." _Ibid._, p. 35. For Dom Stolz' interpretation, refer to _Zur Theologie Anselms in Proslogion_, trans. by A. C. McGill, "Anselm's Theology in the _Proslogion_" in The _Many-Faced Argument_, ed. by Hick and McGill (New York: Macmillan, 1967), pp. 183-206.

5. _Oratio_, (_Opera_ III), 16, 88.

6. _Epistola de Incarnatione Verbi_ I (Opera II), 10, 1-4.

7. _Cur Deus Homo_ (_Opera_ II), 47, 8-9ff.

8. _Proslogion, prooemium_ (_Opera_ II), 93, 21-94, 2.

9. _Epistola_ 345 (_Opera_ V); 283, 24-27.

10. _Epistola_ 112 (_Opera_ III); 246, 74-77.

11. Aristotle, _Metaphysics_, 2, 1; 993b, 19-20ff. 1-2; 982b 27. Refer to a simple direct presentation in Josef Pieper, _Verteidigungsrede für die Philosophie_ (Munich: Kosel-Verlag), trans. A. Lator Ros, _Defensa de la Filosofia_ (Barcelona: Editorial Herder, 1973), esp. pp. 45-93.

12. _Idem._

13. Aquinas, _In Metaphysica_, 2, 1; No. 290. See also No. 297.

14. Leclerq, _Love of Learning_, p. 106.

15. H. Rochais, "_Ipsa philosophia Christus_," _Mediaeval Studies_ (1951), pp. 244-247.

16. Leclercq, <u>Op</u>. <u>cit</u>., p. 108.

17. <u>De</u> <u>Trinitate</u>, 1, 17; 1, 20.

18. <u>Ibid</u>., <u>Tract</u>. <u>in</u> <u>Ioan</u>. CXXIV, 5.

19. Refer to <u>Moralia</u>, 10, 13; 8, 49-50; 31, 101; in <u>Ezech</u>. I,
    10, 26; in <u>Evangelia</u>, 14.4. Competent discussion of this
    aspect of Gregory in Leclercq, Vandenbroucke, and Bouyer, <u>La</u>
    <u>Spiritualité</u> <u>du</u> <u>Moyen</u> <u>Age</u>, trans. by Benedictines of Holme
    Eden Abbey, <u>The</u> <u>Spirituality</u> <u>of</u> <u>the</u> <u>Middle</u> <u>Ages</u> (London:
    Burns and Oats, 1968), pp. 3-31. Also Dom Cuthbert Butler,
    <u>Western</u> <u>Mysticism</u> (London: Arrow, 1960), pp. 124-154.

20. Pieper, <u>op</u>. <u>cit</u>., pp. 60-61.

21. <u>Colossians</u> 2, 8-10. <u>The</u> <u>New</u> <u>English</u> <u>Bible</u> (London: O. U.P.;
    1970). The translation of <u>The</u> <u>Jerusalem</u> <u>Bible</u> is rather
    curious: "Make sure that no one traps you and deprives you
    of your freedom by some secondhand, empty, rational philo-
    sophy, based on the principles of this world instead of on
    Christ." <u>The</u> <u>New</u> <u>Testament</u> (Garden City: Doubleday, 1969).

22. Jerome talls of a dream in which, appearing before the judge-
    ment seat of Christ, he heard the words "Thou a Christian!
    You are a Ciceronian! Where the heart is, there is its
    treasure!" <u>Epist</u>. <u>XXII</u> <u>ad</u> <u>Eustochium</u>, Par. 29, 30. Cited
    in Henry O. Taylor, <u>The</u> <u>Emergence</u> <u>of</u> <u>Christian</u> <u>Culture</u> <u>in</u> <u>the</u>
    <u>West</u> (New York: Harper, 1958), p. 109.

23. <u>De</u> <u>Praescriptionibus</u> <u>Adversus</u> <u>Hereticos</u>, VII, X; cited in H.
    O. Taylor, <u>The</u> <u>Emergence</u> <u>of</u> <u>Christian</u> <u>Culture</u> <u>in</u> <u>the</u> West
    (New York: Harper, 1958), p. 110.

24. <u>De</u> <u>Utilitate</u> <u>Credendi</u>, 9, 22; <u>Sermo</u>. 112, 5; <u>De</u> <u>Vera</u> <u>Reli-</u>
    <u>gione</u>, 49, 94; <u>Confesiones</u> II, 6, 13; et al.

25. Cited in Leclercq, <u>Love</u> <u>of</u> <u>Learning</u>, p. 204.

26. Josef Pieper, <u>The</u> <u>Timelessness</u> <u>and</u> <u>Timeliness</u> <u>of</u> <u>the</u> <u>Cardinal</u>
    <u>Virtues</u> (London: Netherhall House, 1974) pp. 21-22.

27. Martin Heidegger, <u>Sein</u> <u>und</u> <u>Zeit</u> (Seventh edition, Tubingen:
    Neomarius Verlag), translated by J. Macquarrie and E. Robin-
    son, <u>Being</u> <u>and</u> <u>Time</u> (New York: Harper & Row, 1962), Section
    36, pp. 214-217, H. 170-173.

28. Pieper, <u>loc</u>. <u>cit</u>.

29. Aimé Forest, F. von Steenberghen, M. De Gandillac, Le Mouvement doctrinale du XIe au XIVe siècle (Paris: Bloud and Gay, 1951), p. 52.

30. Leclercq et al., Spirituality of the Middle Ages, pp. 165-166.

31. Idem., p. 166.

32. Texts in Anselme Stolz, "Das Proslogion des HL. Anselm," in Revue Benedictine, XLVII, (1935), pp. 336-346.

33. Et mendaciter pronuntiat: 'super senes intellexi,' cui non est, familiare quod sequitur: 'quia mandata tua quaesi.' Nimirum hoc ipsum quod dico: qui non crediderit, non intelliget. Nam qui non crediderit non experietur; et qui expertus non fuerit, non cognoscet. Quantum enim rei auditum superat experientia, tantumvincit audientis cognitionem experientis scientia. Epistola de Incarnatione Verbi 1; 9, 3-8.

34. Monologion, LXVIII; 78, 21-29, 5.

35. Ibid., LXX; 80, 15-25.

36. Monologion, LXX; 80, 29-81, 1.

37. De Doctrina Christiana; 1, 3ff; De Trinitate, 10, 10.

38. "Fateor, domine, et gratias ago, quia creasti in me hanc imaginem tuam, ut tui memor te cogitem, te amem." Proslogion I; 100, 12-13.

39. "Patet itaque quia, sicut sola est mens rationalis inter omnes creaturas, quae ad eius investigationem assurgere valeat, ita nihilominus eadem sola est, per quam maxime ipsamet ad eiusdem inventionem proficere queat." Monologion, 66; 77, 17-20.

40. Ibid., 77, 20-24.

41. Ibid., 67; 78, 1-7.

42. Ibid., 68; 79, 6-9.

43. Paul Evdokimov, "L'Aspect Apophatique de l'argument de saint Anselme," in Spicilegium Beccense, pp. 234-258.

44. Henri de Lubac, "Sur le chapitre XIVe du Proslogion," in Ibid., pp. 295-325.

45. Proslogion, XIV; 111, 12-13.

46. Ibid., 111, 14-15.

47. Ibid., XXVI; 120, 25-121, 1.

48. "Rationalem naturam a deo factam esse iustam, ut illo fruendo
    beata esset, dubitari non debet. Ideo namque rationalis est,
    ut discernat inter iustem et iniustum, et inter bonum et
    malum, et inter magis bonum et minus bonum." Cur Deus Homo
    (Opera II), II, 1; 97, 4-7. Also, Ibid., 97, 7-98, 5.

49. "Cur non te sentit, domine deus, anima mea si invenit te."
    Pros., XIV; 111, 14-15.

50. Ibid., XXIV; 118, 2-3.

51. Ibid., XXV; 120, 20.

52. Ibid., XXVI; 121, 14-18.

53. Ibid., XIV; 112, 6-8.

54. Ibid., I; 98, 4-6.

55. Ibid., XVI; 112, 20-113, 4, esp. 112, 27.

56. Ibid., 112, 20-24.

57. Ibid., 113, 2-4.

58. Ibid., XVII; 113, 12-15.

59. Ibid., XVIII; 114, 2.

60. Ibid., 114, 12-13.

61. Responsio, I; 132, 5-7.

62. Ibid., 132, 7-9.

63. De Veritate (Opera I) V; 181, 12-14ff.

64. Ibid., 181, 21-28.

65. Idem.

66. The Writings of Clement of Alexandria, trans. W. Wilson
    (Edinburgh: T&T Clark, 1872), Vol. II, Stromata II, 6: "The
    exercise of faith becomes knowledge, resting on a sure foun-

dation" (p.6) ... "knowledge --- is characterized by faith, and faith, by a kind of divine mutual and reciprocal correspondence, becomes characterized by knowledge." (Id.) ; VI, 7: "Knowledge or wisdom ought to be exercised up to the eternal and unchangeable habit of contemplation" (p. 339); VI, 18: "real science (episteme), which we affirm the Gnostic alone possesses is certain knowledge (cataleksis), leading up through true and sure reasons to the knowledge (gnosis)of the cause (p.401),VII, X: "by starting from this faith, and being displayed by it through the grace of God, the knowledge respecting Him is to be acquired as far as possible" (p. 446). An invaluable study on Clement is found in Paul Dudon, Le Gnostique de Saint Clement d'Alexandrie: Opuscule inédit de Fenelon (Paris: Gabriel Beauchisme, 1930).

67. Nonetheless, the charge levelled against Clement that he believed that man's supreme end is not love but knowledge, tends to emphasize the importance of his Hellenistic background. Refer to R. Mel Wilson, The Gnostic Problem (London: A.R. Mawbray & Co., 1958), p. 134ff. Texts such as Stromata IV, XXII, in which knowledge of God is preferred over salvation and love is considered as the medium of access to knowledge seem to bear out this interpretation. The Writings of Clement, II, p. 202ff.

68. Cur deus Homo, Commendatio; 40, 10-12.

69. "Solent enim quidam cum coeperint quasi cornua confidentis sibi scientiae producere, nescientes quia si quis se existimat scire aliquid, nondum cognovit quemadmodum aporteat eum scire antequam habeant per solidatatem fidei alas spirituales, praesumendo in altissimas de fide quaestiones assurgere." Epistola de Incarnatione Verbi, (Opera II), I; 7, 6-10.

70. See especially, Orationes sive Meditationes (Opera III), prologus; 3, 1-4.

71. Proslogion, XXVI; 120, 25-121, 1.

72. Ibid., 121, 18.

73. Dom Anselme Stolz, op. cit.

74. Ibid., pp. 185-187.

75. Ibid., 198.

76. Note especially Proslogion, Chapters XXII and XXIV: 116, 15-

117, 25-118, 9.

77. <u>Ibid.</u>, 104, 15-16.

78. "Ergo, domine, non solum es quo maius cogitari nequit, sed es quiddam maius quam cogitari possit." <u>Ibid.</u>, XV; 112, 14-15; et al. esp. <u>Proslogion</u> XXII: 116, 15-117, 2. Refer to Sylvia Crocker's 'The Ontological Significance of Anselm's <u>Proslogion</u>' in <u>Modern Schoolman</u>, 50 (Nov., 1972), pp. 33-56.

79. <u>Monologion</u>, esp. chapters 1-3; 13, 1-15, 23.

80. <u>Proslogion</u>, XXII; 22-117, 2.

81. For example, in Southern, <u>St. Anselm and His Biographer</u>, p. 63; et al.

82. <u>Regula</u>, cap. 8, 48, 58.

83. M.D. Chenu, <u>Toward Understanding Saint Thomas</u> (Chicago: Henry Regnery, 1963), p. 81. Refer especially to the second section of Chapter II, pp. 80-96 in which meditation is compared to St. Thomas' procedures of exposition.

84. <u>Didascalion</u>, iii, 10 (ed. Buttiner, p. 59), cited by Southern, <u>op. cit.</u>, p. 53. Another text of Hugh of St. Victor cited by the same author, <u>idem</u>, note 3: "Meditatio acuit ingenium, ingenium rationem; ratio conducit ad intellectum, intellectus ad intelligentiam, intelligentia per contemplationem ipsam veritatem admiratur, et per caritatem in ea delectatur."

85. Quentin Lauer, "Hegel on Proofs for God's Existence" in <u>Kant-Studien</u> (Köln: Kölner Universitäts-Verlag, 1964), Band 55, Heft 4; pp. 443-465, esp. p. 457.

CHAPTER VI

MEDIEVAL AND MODERN CRITICISM

Gaunilo's critique of the _Proslogion_ argument occupies a
deservedly unique position in Anselmian studies. Unlike many of
his successors, Gaunilo is familiar with Anselm's text and does
not have to rely on distorted versions of the argument. He has
kind words for the bulk of the argument, centering his attack on
those initial chapters, _Proslogion_ II - III, which in his opinion,
are rightly sensed but lacking rigorous demonstration.[1] His
criticism is incisive and in spite of Anselm's _Responsio_, assuredly a tour de force, cannot be lightly dismissed. Gaunilo
can be faulted only with a certain impatience which may account
for his (at times) improper rendering of the argument, and his
failure to grasp the nuances implicit in his own critique. Perhaps this is too much to ask from a mere five pages in the critical edition, which undoubtedly has the merit of addressing itself
to the weaker aspects of the argument and setting the stage for
further criticism.

Gaunilo begins by restating the argument. The existence of
a nature-than-which-nothing-greater-can-be-thought is demonstrated by (a) the fact that the 'doubter' already has it in his
mind as he understands (_intelligit_) what is said, and (b) this
nature is necessarily such that it exists not only in the mind but in
reality, as (c) it is greater to exist both in the mind and reality than in the mind alone.[2] This is, as far as it goes, a
rather weak but not erroneous paraphrase of Anselm's _Proslogion_
II argument. Gaunilo continues, "for if this same being exists
in the mind alone, anything that existed also in reality would
be greater than this being and thus that which is greater than
everything (_maius omnibus_) would be less than some thing and not
greater than everything, which is obviously contradictory".[3]

This text is important in that we find Anselm's description
of God as '_aliquid-quo-maius-nihil-cogitari-potest_' modified to
'_maius omnibus_'. Furthermore, Anselm does not compare 'something-than-which-nothing-greater-can-be-thought' with other
beings, but bases his argument on its own inner exigencies
grounded on the principle of contradiction. He does not attempt
to prove that it would be less than other real beings if existence _in re_ were denied it but rather that denial of real existence would entail a contradiction.

In any event, the argument, as reproduced by Gaunilo, bears sufficient similarity to the original for it and the ensuing critique to be taken seriously. He begins by indicating that 'this being' can be said to exist in the mind only insofar as what is said is understood. This would apply equally well to a fiction.[4] It follows that Anselm must demonstrate that 'something-than-which-nothing-greater-can-be-thought' is to be distinguished from purely fictional entities. He must prove by 'certain knowledge' that the thing itself actually exists, "nisi intelligendo id est scientia comprehendendo re ipsa illud existere".[5] This he cannot do as then there would be no difference between thinking an object and understanding that it exists,[6] between the concept and the existence of a thing: anything thought of would exist in re. As this is not the case, Anselm is obliged to prove that there is something, which, as soon as it is thought of, cannot be entertained by the mind except as indubitably existing, "it must already be in my mind when I understand what I hear".[7]

Anselm's example of the painter contradicts his own position. A picture before it is painted exists in the art of the painter, "nihil est aliud quam pars quaedam intelligentiae ipsius".[8] As there is a distinction between truth and the mind which apprehends it[9] it would seem that 'something-than-which-nothing-greater-can-be-thought' is either part of the 'furniture' of the mind or it is not. If it is not then Anselm's proof does not hold. It would possess no privileged status and be reduced to one among a multiplicity of thinkable things. On the contrary, if it belongs to the very nature of the mind, then other more properly theological objections could be brought to bear. In later times the accusation would take the form of 'ontologism', a charge often levelled against Anselm.[10] Gaunilo, however, at this point, is content to point out the inappropriateness of the example of the painter.

Centering on the special status which he gives to 'aliquid-omnibus-maius' Gaunilo suggests that it can not be thought of any more than can God Himself, "for neither do I know the reality itself, nor can I form an idea from some other thing like it, since, as you yourself state, it is such that nothing could be like it".[11] To speak about the unknown, one is forced to use terms derived from those things which are known, included under genus and species. But as God is not subsumed under genus and species there appears to be no point of departure for any possible knowledge about Him. You can think of a man who does not exist in reality because you arleady know what a man is. Although you may be mistaken about the existential status of this or that man you possess a solid base from which to initiate your investigations. But, insofar as 'deus' or 'aliquid-omnibus-maius' are concerned, one is limited to the verbal formula and on this

shaky ground one can hardly proceed further.[12] Although sounds
are heard their meaning remains unknown as the thing itself is
not known.[13]

   As 'aliquid-omnibus-maius' cannot be thought of in a unique
way, if it exists in the mind at all, it exists in precisely the
same way as all other things.[14] From the premise that 'something-
greater-than-everying' exists in the mind in this blanket fashion
it is gratuitous to conclude to real existence, which must be
demonstrated by rigorous argument.[15] But there is no such argument, only a laborious effort to imagine something which, on the
basis of the spoken words alone, is completely unknown.[16] Even
this effort is based on the premise that 'maius-omnibus' exists
in the mind, a premise which can be doubted or denied.[17] Moreover, the opaque mental existence given fictions can be denied
to 'something-greater-than-anything' as mere words do not necessarily reflect conceptual existence. Instead of vaulting from
conceptual to real existence it must first be demonstrated that
this 'greater-than-everything' exists somewhere in reality. Only
then will its character of being greater than everything lead to
an affirmation of its a se existence.[18]

   This is a deft criticism aimed at the Achilles' heel of
Anselm's argument. If even conceptual existence is denied to
'aliquid-quo-nihil-maius-cogitari-possit', the movement of the
argument is aborted. If it is granted,then criticism will focus
on the transition from the conceptual to the real order, objections which have glutted Proslogion criticism. This objection is
made by Gaunilo in his 'lost island' example. It is fallacious
to conclude to the existence of an island, blessed with all possible riches and delights, solely from its notion.[19] The example
is unfortunate, as the 'lost island' is not a valid analogue for
'that-than-which-a-greater-cannot-be-thought', and weakens his
rebuttal. In any event, Gaunilo insists that if the existence
of 'omnibus-maius' is not assumed then the argument of Proslogion
III is unacceptable.[20]

   Even if the existence of 'omnibus-maius' is granted and
Anselm's conclusion sound, it would still be better to say that
it cannot be understood (intelligi) not to exist, instead of
stating that it cannot be thought (cogitari) not to exist.
Strictly speaking, unreal things cannot be understood although
they can be thought, in the way that the Fool thought that God
does not exist.[21] It is Gaunilo's contention that God's unique
noetic characteristic is not to be understood not to exist.[22] As
Gaunilo had previously defined understanding as "scientia comprehendendo re ipsa illud existere",[23] his contention is anticli-
matic.

   Gaunilo makes some telling points. Anselm seem to be using

91

a formula which is so nebulous that even conceptual existence is in doubt, one which, not determined by genus and species, can have little or no meaning. Even if existence in the mind were granted it would be an existence common to fictions and other unreal things. From this basis it would be impossible to arrive at real existence. The only way to flesh Anselm's description and solve the conundrum of the completely unknown 'being-greater-than-everything' is to prove that it really exists. Once exist- ence in re is established, then existence in intellectu assumes the privileged and certain character proposed by Anselm.

Anselm's Responsio

Anselm's reply to Gaunilo is a classic which, in spite of its acuity, does not obviate the force of his critique. Answer- ing the catholicus instead of the insipiens, Anselm indicates that if a being 'than-which-a-greater-cannot-be-thought' is neither understood nor thought it would follow that (1) God is not that being 'than-which-a-greater-cannot-be-thought' or (2) God is not in the mind or thought, "non est in intellectu vel cogitatione".[24] But neither conclusions can be entertained by a Christian: so Anselm's strongest argument is made to "fides et conscientia tua".[25] The remainder of the small treaties is dedi- cated to refuting Gaunilo on the thematic level; if 'that-than- which-a-greater-can-not-be-thought'is thought, it exists in reality: "si vel cogitari potest esse, necesse est illud esse".[26]

Anselm tries to prove that 'something-than-which-a-greater- cannot-be-thought' is not on the same level as other entities, both those that enjoy real existence and those whose existence is limited to the mind. It cannot be thought of except without a beginning, while fictions,although they can be thought of as existing,must be thought of as having a beginning to their exist- ence. Furthermore, 'that-than-which-a-greater-cannot-be-thought' exists as a whole at every time and every place.[27] These pecu- liar characteristics distinguish 'that-than-which-a-greater-can- not-be-thought' not only from mental fictions but also from real things, which, having a beginning and an end, are spatio-temporal, composed of parts, and can be thought not to exist.[28] Insofar as 'that-than-which-a-greater-cannot-be-thought' is concerned, its privileged status is guaranteed: if it is thought, it is neces- sary that it exist.

Even if the existence of this being were doubted, one would have to admit that were it to exist it would exist necessarily: in Anselm's words, "it would not be capable of not-existing either actually or in the mind".[29] Otherwise, a greater could be thought and it would not be 'that-than-which-a-greater-cannot-be-

thought' As 'that-than-which-a-greater-cannot-be-thought' cannot
be thought not to exist, it is distinguished from fictional entities as well as from really existing things, and the same conclusion is reached: if it is thought, it is necessary that it
exist.[30] An outright denial its existence would entail that it
could be thought of as a contingent being, and this is not possible.[31] Therefore, Gaunilo's denial, like that of the Fool of
the Proslogion, is on the level of mere words, not on the level
of understanding.

Broaching the objection that though the words of the formula are understood its referent can not really be considered as
possessing conceptual existence, Anselm counters that we do understand something concerning it, those characteristic previously
discussed: it exists as a whole in any place and time, has no
beginning nor end, is not composed of parts. It exists 'in intellectu' to the extent that we understand that it possesses these
characteristics.[32] It suffices for the God-description to be
spoken in a familiar language and heard by the Fool in order for
him to understand it, and what is understood is in the mind.[33]
It cannot be in the mind alone as 'that-than-which-a-greater-
cannot-be-thought' would then be 'that-than-which-a-greater-can-
be-thought'.[34] Once again, the same conclusion follows: if it
exists in the mind, it also exists in reality.

Anselm appreciated the force of this objection. He returns
to it and its solution several times in the course of the Responsio. Against Gaunilo's contention that 'that-than-which-a-
greater-cannot-be-thought' cannot be thought (cogitari) or in the
mind (in intellectu) as the thing-itself cannot be known nor any
notion of it formed, Anselm counters that conjecture is possible
starting from the good found in things, ascending from the less
to the more good, from those things than-which-something-greater-
can-be-thought to that being 'than-which-a-greater-cannot-be-
thought.'[35] A tenuous notion may be formed of God. Although
existence in the mind, is,in Gaunilo's opinion, merely a blanket
term covering unreal or doubtfully real things, and leads nowhere,
for Anselm it is a convenient point of departure.[36] It can be
understood to some extent and provide the basis for demonstration.[37]

The reality signified by the description and the description
itself are certainly different. Even if the reality, 'that-than-
which-a-greater-cannot-be-thought', could not be thought of
(cogitari) nor understood (intelligi), the description could be
thought of and understood.[38] The word 'ineffable' is understood
without knowing what is said to be ineffable. The very denial
of the existence of 'that-than-which-a-greater-cannot-be-thought'
presupposes a minimal understanding of what is being denied.[39]
With regard to this being, thinking and understanding fuse: there

is a <u>cogitari</u> which is also an <u>intelligi</u>.[40] To think of 'that-
than-which-a-greater-cannot-be-thought', is to think of something
that cannot not exist, and therefore exists necessarily.[41]

Gaunilo is taken to task for affirming that it would be better to say that the supreme reality cannot be understood not to
exist, rather than it cannot be thought not to exist. But, as
nothing that exists can be understood not to exist, this cannot
be the distinguishing characteristic of God,[42] as He would be
included among all existing things. However, all beings except
God--under the description 'that-than-which-a-greater-cannot-be-
thought'--can be thought of as not existing.[43] Also, Gaunilo's
use of understanding is imprecise. He believes both that unreal
things are understood and that understanding signifies knowing
with certainty that something actually exists,[44] an obvious contradiction. In addition, the argument has not been reproduced
correctly: '<u>maius omnibus</u>' and '<u>quo-maius-cogitari-nequit</u>' are
different, not equivalent for proving the existence of God.[45]
After all,'<u>maius omnibus</u>', should it exist, could still be thought
of as not existing.[46] It would have to be reduced to '<u>quo-maius-
cogitari-nequit</u>' in order to be incorporated into the argument.
On the contrary, '<u>quo-maius-cogitari-nequit</u>' cannot be understood
except as that which is greater than everything.[47]

Although Anselm ends his <u>Responsio</u> with the statement that,
in spite of Gaunilo's objections, his argument has not been weakened but demonstrated by rigorous argumentation,[48] the exchange
is somewhat unsettling. If Anselm has shown himself the superior
thinker the impression remains that his defense is flawed, that
he relies far too much on dialectical pyrotechnics. He succeeds
in refuting the charge that his God-description is arbitrary,
possessing no conceptual reality, but deals less rigorously with
the charge indicating an illicit transition between the conceptual and real orders. At times, Gaunilo is his own worst enemy,
as when he follows an insightful critique -that '<u>maius omnibus</u>'
can be denied conceptual existence- with his banal example of the
'lost island'. This faltering is taken advantage of by Anselm,
to the point of overshadowing the better points of Gaunilo's
critique.

Perhaps the most important aspect of the exchange is
Gaunilo's emphasis on God as a reality that cannot be understood
to exist contrasted to Anselm's emphasis on God as a reality that
can not be thought not to exist. As indicated previously, thinking (<u>cogitare</u>) represents the active element within cognition,
primarily linked with the possible, while understanding (<u>intel-
ligere</u>) represents the passive element, the contact between the
mind and reality. Anselm's refutation of Gaunilo on this point
covers the movement of the argument from the possible to the real.
The exigencies of the possible -that '<u>quo-maius-cogitari-nequit</u>'

cannot be thought not to exist- determines the structure of the real order. God's necessity extends to the very limits of possibility.

Gaunilo's critique is directed against the first sections of the _Proslogion_. He had only kind words for the bulk of the argument, which very probably corresponded to the spiritual ambiance of the times, shared by himself and Anselm. The hiatus in _Proslogion_ criticism from Gaunilo's critique to William of Auxerre's _Summa Aurea_, written between 1215 and 1231, has been attributed to its status as a devotional tract and the consequent undervaluing of its speculative aspect. A further contributing cause could have been the displacement of the center of culture from the monastery to the cathedral school and university, the transition from monastic to scholastic culture. Whatever the case may be the argument does reach the thirteenth century in the desiccated form presented in the _Summa Aurea_, as Chatillon's says "reduced to a purely rational scholastic argument".[49] He is correct in suggesting that the _Proslogion_ argument, when fitted into the world of the _Summae_, loses its proper character.

Thomas Aquinas

Aquinas takes Gaunilo's critique one step further, covering the argument under the heading: _Utrum Deum esse sit per se notum_.[50] It almost seems that we are dealing with a further elaboration _pro insipiente_. Aquinas' argument is to the point: as it is impossible to think (_cogitare_) the opposite of self-evident truth and God's non-existence can be thought (e.g., the Fool), it follows that God's existence is not self-evident.[51] He distinguishes between two ways in which a proposition can be self-evident (its predicate included in the concept of the subject): (1) in itself but not in respect to us, (2) in itself and in respect to us. Insofar as God is concerned the proposition 'God exists' is self-evident in itself, God is His own being,but it is not self-evident to us as we do not know the divine nature. Therefore God's existence must be demonstrated by means of things which are known to us, i.e. by effects.[52] Because of this, _propter quid_ demonstration, which proceeds from cause to effect, cannot be used to prove the existence of God. Only _quia_ demonstration, which proceeds from effect to cause, can be employed: "_Unde Deum esse, secundum quod non est per se notum quoad nos, demonstrabile est per effectus nobis notos_".[53]

The second difficulty to the first article of the _Summa_ contains a paraphrase of the _Proslogion_ argument:[54] once the meaning of the word '_Deus_' is understood, God's existence is immediately apprehended, since this name signifies "_id quo maius significari_ non <u>potest</u>", and that which exists both in the mind and reality is greater than that which exists in the mind alone. Aquinas objects that it is possible for '<u>Deus</u>' not to be understood in this way as some have even believed God to be a body. Furthermore, even if it is understood in this way it would not entail real existence but only mental existence. Real existence can be demonstrated only by assuming it in the first place. Aquinas sidesteps Anselm's position by affirming that the point of departure of the argument is the meaning of the word '<u>Deus</u>' as we cannot know God's nature. The usual ground of demonstration '<u>quid est</u>', must be replaced by '<u>quid significet nomen</u>'. Further, God's names are derived from His effects, and so the possibility of a <u>quia</u> demonstration is established. It is necessary to first answer the question '<u>an est</u>' before broaching the question '<u>quid est</u>'.[55] But Anselm's assertion that God is that then which nothing greater can be thought is hardly equivalent to saying that the word '<u>Deus</u>' means 'that-than-which-nothing-greater-can-be-thought'.

The critique of the argument is instructive as it serves to illustrate the unpleasant fate that awaits any speculation served from its roots and inserted into an alien framework. Aquinas' thought is impervious to the argument. Although he admits that there exists in man a certain confused knowledge of God's existence this is only in the sense that God is man's beatitude.[56] Even in regard to the '<u>imago dei</u>', while admitting that the <u>Deus Trinitas</u> made man in his image, and citing Augustine to the effect that it is reflected in man's ability to remember, understand, and love God, St. Thomas will dwell on the weakness of the relationship "<u>sicut denarius dicitur imago Caesaris, inquantum habet Caesaris imaginem</u>'.[57]

While following the gloss in distinguishing a triple image of God in man, (1) <u>creatio</u>: given in all men; (2) <u>recreatio</u>: given only in the just; and (3) <u>similitudo</u>; given exclusively in the blessed, Aquinas does not proceed to discuss the continuity that may exists between them.[58] Only in the "<u>sancti qui sunt in patria</u>" does he specifically note the transformation from glory to glory of <u>Corinthians</u> II.[59] Again, although the mind can use reason to know God as His image is imprinted on the mind,[60] the approach through interiority is not suggested. God can be known only in His role as first cause of all things, through His effects, which corresponds to our human mode of knowing based on sense experience.[61]

Aquinas' conception of reason and the relation between faith and reason is different from Anselm as is their point of departure for demonstration. For Anselm, as most Augustinians, there is no clear distinction between philosophy and theology: to separate knowledge from wisdom would render both impossible undertakings. St. Thomas, on the other hand, conceives nature and reason as open to the supernatural, but not as organically related to it. What for Anselm is a unitary movement towards the fruition of God, is found, in Aquinas, in a discrete and compartmentalized form. Philosophy may well, as Maritain states,"engender in the soul a certain velleity it is unable to satisfy, a confused and indeterminate desire for a higher knowledge",[62] but to arrive at this higher knowledge it is necessary to switch tracks, to forge into another domain. Not to do so would be to confuse the orders of grace and nature.[63] Whether or not Aquinas is precisely reflected in the views of Maritain, it is nevertheless true that he continues the tradition of the Summa Aurea by presenting the argument in a desiccated form, reducing it to the per se notum plea, and limiting it to a somewhat arbitrary rendition of Proslogion II.

His critique, whatever the historical mabiguities involved, does not altogether miss the mark. As with Gaunilo, the bone of contention here is the adequacy of 'something-than-which-a-greater-cannot-be-thought' as a name of God. But we are not debating within a more or less accepted universe of discourse as seems to be the case with Gaunilo. There are two substantially different views about man, knowledge, and reality. Only by recognizing this, can the argument and it's critique be evaluated.

Duns Scotus

Duns Scotus seems to have favored Anselm's argument but found it in need of completion, and therefore presented several 'colorings' or restatements. Perhaps the most interesting 'coloring' is found in his Ordinatio, that is, his Oxford Commentary on the Sentences of Peter Lombard. Duns Scotus' argument can be reduced to the following syllogism: if God (ens infinitum) is possible, He exists. God is possible. Therefore, He exists.[64] He has completed ('colored') the argument by equating 'something-than-which-nothing-greater-can-be-thought' with infinite being, and proving that this greatest thinkable object is possible as it can be thought without contradiction. Only in such an object is the intellect fully satisfied.[65] To deny it real existence would entail a contradiction: if God were merely possible, He would depend on another being, and would no longer be God. He would both exist qua possible and not-exist, as subordinate to another cause.[66] Therefore, if such a being can be thought without contradiction it is possible and if it is possible it exists in reality.

Duns Scotus attempts to complete the Proslogion argument within the context of his own thought, which is unfortunately,as

Bréhier has noted, diametrically opposed to Anselm's <u>credo ut</u>
<u>intelligam</u>.[67] While Anselm unearths necessary reasons, Scotus
extends the list of <u>credibilia</u>. Moreover, the argument can be
faulted even on Scotist grounds, the doctrine of univocity of
being presenting especial difficulties. This being which is
thought of as common to God and creature is the being neither of
God nor of creatures. The very fact that many of Scotus' demonstrations start from being simply emphasizes that this concept is
not the concept of God. Otherwise, there could be nothing to
prove. Furthermore, as the infinite is understood through the
finite, the human mind can scarcely grasp the relation between
infinity and being, though it may conclude that an infinite being
is not an absurdity and it's possibility cannot be discarded <u>a</u>
<u>priori</u>. Perhaps Scotus, as Bettoni contends, believed that the
Anselmian argument, even 'colored', was simply a <u>persuasio</u> (a
persuasive argument) and not a demonstration.[68]

                              Descartes

     Aquinas and Duns Scotus mark the first stage of the meta-
morphosis of the <u>Proslogion</u> argument into that ectoplasmic 'ontological' argument which has become a dependable staple of our
histories of philosophy. Descartes '<u>a priori</u>' demonstration
-usually considered as a legitimate offshoot and certainly the
'ontological' argument <u>par excellence</u> of modern and contemporary
philosophy- illustrates a further transformation. It differs in
content, method, style, and inspiration. While Anselm presents a
single argument which requires no further grounding than itself
alone, Descartes appears to base his <u>a priori</u> demonstration on
the <u>a posteriori</u> proof of the third meditation. The latter establishes it's major premise: "that which we clearly understand to
belong to the nature of anything can be truly affirmed of that
thing".[69] All clear and distinct ideas are true as God, who is
veracious, produces them. To think of God, the supremely perfect
being, as lacking existence, would be as absurd as to think of
a mountain without a valley. But the primacy of the <u>a posteriori</u>
demonstration is stated explicitly by Descartes: the proof
through effects is the principal demonstration "<u>ne dicam unicam</u>"
of God's existence.[70] Descartes insists in both the second and
fourth <u>Replies</u> that his point of departure is the existence of
God demonstrated by reasons, that is, the demonstration through
effects.[71]

     This conclusion is further supported by the importance Des-
cartes gives to the notion of God as <u>causa sui</u>, a notion vigor-
ously opposed by Arnauld in the fourth set of objections. Aware
that this was Arnauld's main objection,[72] Descartes counters by
insisting on the importance of including even God Himself under

                               98

the rubric of efficient causality. If self-derived existence were interpreted as lacking a cause there would be no reason by which to prove God's existence from His effects.... hence we must in no account sanction it".[73] Therefore, the non-causal interpretation of self-derivation must be rejected. As efficient causality deals with the existence of a thing, were God to be excluded the main force of the present argument and of all demonstration would be lost.[74] Descartes defense of the notion of God as <u>causa sui</u> is more impressive than the notion itself. As Heidegger notes, "before the <u>causa sui</u> man cannot fall on his knees in awe; in the presence of a God like this, he cannot make music and dance".[75] Anselm's notion of God is far closer to the God of revelation.

The <u>Proslogion</u> is an organic whole, in which spiritual purification and prayer are joined with dialectics and speculation in the quest for God. It is a praying in thought directed towards the contemplation of God, emulating, on the level of interiority, the pilgrimage of medieval piety. The <u>Meditations</u> is not fundamentally a religious work. Anselm encounters God as the outcome of intellectual and spiritual ascesis. Descartes encounters Him on a purely cognitive level. The apprehension of the infinite and perfect by means of clear and distinct ideas is possible because of the absence of extraneous religious factors. Arnauld took Descartes to task for omitting the moral and religious domains from methodic doubt. Why does Descartes center on the mistakes made in distinguishing between true and false, and not on the errors made distinguishing good from evil?[76] Stressing intelligence, Descartes seems to ignore those things which deal with faith and the conduct of life.[77] Descartes admits the charge while insisting that even the domains of religion and morality are also under the aegis of reason.[78]

The <u>Proslogion</u> illustrates the movement of the whole man to his transcendent source, a dynamism which mediates between the human condition and the beatific vision. Descartes is primarily engaged in his attempt to discover the Archimedean point to base certitude, particularly, the world as <u>res extensa</u>. He considered that God is almost transparently present in the human mind, that the notion of God is prior to the notion of myself.[79] The work of understanding is not impeded, as it is for Anselm, by residues of original sin, but rather by 'prejudices', especially the prejudices of the senses.[80] While Anselm's argument encompasses the whole man, Descartes' <u>a priori</u> demonstration is based on a double reduction: the whole man is reduced to <u>res cogitans</u>, and this in turn, to a single <u>cogitatum</u>.[81]

The idea of God contains all thinkable perfections and is compared by Descartes to the mark of the workman imprinted on his work.[82] Once thought this idea cannot be expanded syntheti-

cally. Though new perfections may be detected this only serves
to make the original conception distinct and explicit. In Descartes' words, the idea of God "is not found by us _seriatim_ by
amplifying the perfections of created things but is constituted
as a whole at one time".[83] Although this idea does not give us
adequate knowledge of God it suffices to let us know that He
exists.[84] The key to Descartes' conception of God is the idea
of infinity, and this is not found in Anselm. Duns Scotus first
it. For Descartes, God alone is infinite, that in which nowhere
are limits to be found.[85] God is not greater than can be thought
by us as He is conceived as infinite and nothing can be greater
than the infinite.[86] While Anselm stresses Divine Unity, Descartes stresses Divine Power, an attribute which grounds the
solution of the _causa_ _sui_ issue. God's inexhaustible power is
the reason why He requires no cause other than Himself.[87] Necessary existence itself is comprised in the idea of a being of
the highest power.[88]

We must conclude that any interpretation of the _Proslogion_
argument through Cartesian perspective would probably be defective. To view both arguments as different variations on a common
theme may also be unwarranted. Because of this it is risky to
consider the attacks launched against Descartes' _a priori_ demonstration as applying equally to the _Proslogion_ argument. None
the less,it is clear that immunity from prosecution cannot be
granted to either argument.

                              Kant

Kant's criticism bears consideration if only because of the
enormous influence it has exercised which is reflected in its
status as the the final solution to the 'ontological' argument,
for many, its definitive refutation. Although Kant considers
that there are three paths in which a rational demonstration of
God's existence may be attempted, the physico-theological, the
cosmological, and the ontological, the latter, which argues completely _a priori_ from mere concepts, is the first to be studied
in the first _Kritik_.[89] Inverting the 'natural process' of reasoning which is to proceed from the empirical to the transcendental, Kant first broaches the ontological proof because it
marks the _goal_ of reason and all other demonstrations must ultimately recur to it for their fulfillment.[90]

The ontological argument begins with a 'mere' idea, the concept of an absolutely necessary being, defined as "something the
non-existence of which is impossible."[91] This verbal definition
gives little insight into the conditions which account for its
necessity, which must be known to determine whether anything is

really thought. Examples such as the triangle having three angles are taken from judgments not things and "the absolute necessity of the judgment is only a conditioned necessity of the
thing".[92] Necessity follows from the very existence of the triangle. In both triangle and the absolute necessary being existence has been arbitrarily included in the concept. The triangle,
if it exists, has three angles. God, if He exists, exists necessarily. If the existence of the thing is rejected all its predicates are also rejected. If the existence of God is rejected all
His attributes are also rejected. As Kant indicates it is impossible "to form the least concept of a thing, which, should it be
rejected with all its predicates, leaves behind a contradiction."[93]

     The 'ontological' argument as understood by Kant argues from
the logical possibility of concepts to the real existence of the
thing as follows: as 'all reality' includes existence if this
thing is rejected it's internal possibility is also rejected,
which is self-contradictory.[94] But since all existential propositions are synthetic, it is possible to reject the predicate of
existence without falling into a contradiction.[95] In confusing
a logical predicate with a real predicate, a concept that en-
larges the concept of a thing, an illusion is generated which
leads to error. The point is illustrated in his example of the
hundred thalers, the gist of which is that "the object, as it
actually exists, is not analytically contained in my concept, but
is added to my concept....synthetically".[96] Nothing is added to
a thing when we assert that it exists.

     The reverse is also true. The mere concept of a thing does
not entail its existence: "even if I think a being as the supreme
reality, without any defect, the question still remains whether
it exists or not".[97] Existence belongs to the unity of experience
and any presumed existence which is not included can neither be
demonstrated nor declared impossible.[98] Although the concept of
a Supreme Being is certainly useful it is a 'mere idea' and cannot extend our knowledge to include either the existence or pos-
sibility-of-existence of anything beyond what is known through
experience.[99] The connection of real properties belongs to synthesis alone and the criterion of synthesis is experience. This
'unfortunate' proof, "which yields satisfaction neither to the
natural and healthy understanding nor to the more academic demands of strict proof" should be discarded.[100] As both the
Physico-Theological and the Cosmological proofs require the Ontological proof for their completion to disprove the latter is to
disprove the former. This is to say ,there are no definitive
proofs for the existence of God.

     To make sense out of the rather sketchy outline given above
one should note that Kant believed that a 'mere idea' was less

real than a category. The categories, as they are applied to the sensible manifold, can be exhibited in concreto, while ideas find no appearance in which they can be exhibited, as they surpass the scope of any possible empirical knowledge. Kant compares them to the Platonic ideas: they possess practical power as regulative principles, and form the basis of the possible perfections of certain actions.[101] He further distinguishes between the 'idea', which gives the rule, and the 'ideal,' which serves as the archetype for the complete determination of the copy. While virtue, human wisdom in its complete purity is an 'idea', the wise man of the Stoics would be the 'ideal'.[102] Ideals do not possess objective reality but they are not mere fictions of the imagination. Although they cannot be imagined or depicted in any way they rest on determinate concepts and serve as a rule of action. In the ideal, reason aims at complete determination in accordance with a priori rules.[103]

God is the Ideal of Reason. Each thing may be considered in relation to the sum-total of all possibilities. Considered as an a priori condition, all things may be said to derive their possibility through their participation in the sum of all possibilities which is their common correlate.[104] Through the principle of determinability, certain incompatible predicates are excluded from the idea of the sum-total of all possibilities and it then becomes the concept of "an individual object which is completely determined through the mere idea, and must therefore be entitled an ideal of pure reason".[105] This substrate, then, which contains the storehouse of all possibilities, is transformed from a mere representation, the concept of the Ens realissimum, into an object, is then hypostatized, and finally personified as God.[106]

The Ideal of Reason, is merely an idea, not an existing being, the prototypon or archetype from which all imperfect copies (ectypa) derive the material of their possibility. Similar to the Platonic Ideas, things approximate it without exhausting its possibility. The Idea of Reason is no more than a mere fiction in which we combine and realize the manifold of our idea in an ideal as an individual being.[107] It is produced by a natural illusion, based on the principle that nothing is an object for us unless it presupposes the sum of all empirical reality as the condition for its possibility.[108] Kant seems to postulate a drive which propels the mind from the conditioned to the unconditioned, which, though unreal, provides the ground for the conditions of all things. The illusion is natural. Even the 'least reflective' of men take this course.[109]

Kant's rejection of the 'ontological' proof rests on two propositions. First, that it makes an illicit transition from the mere idea of an absolutely necessary being (something the

non-existence of which is impossible) to its existence. A mere
idea cannot extend our knowledge to include the existence or pos-
sibility-of-existence of anything beyond what is known in experience. The concept of a thing does not entail its existence.
The connection of real properties belongs to synthesis. Secondly,
existence is not a predicate as nothing is added to a thing when
we affirm that it exists. Does this criticism apply to the Proslogion argument?

Kant was probably unaware of it's original formulation.
Koyré suggests that even though Kant attributed the 'ontological'
argument to Descartes, the one he criticized was Leibniz' as
formulated by Christian Wolff.[110] However this may be, the proof
criticized by Kant differs from the Proslogion argument. To begin with, Anselm does not postulate 'something-than-which-nothing-
greater-can-be-thought' as a mere idea, constituted as a whole at
one time. It may be uncovered seriatim, mounting from the less
to the more good. It is questionable whether the argument is
'ontological' in Kant's sense. The Proslogion argument does not
use as its point of departure the notion of an absolutely necessary being, but builds up to it. Finally, the progressive development of the argument as found in the Proslogion is missing in
the proof criticized by Kant. Whether this compressed 'ontological' proof may be identified with Anselm's argument is doubt-
ful. The argument certainly proceeds from logical possibility
to real existence. But is this transition possible? The Proslogion argument does not proceed directly from the logical possibility of concepts to the real existence of things but rather
from logical possibility to logical necessity and only then to
necessary existence. As Malcolm has indicated, the whole of the
argument is that if the description of God is properly understood,
it is evident that one cannot reject the subject.[111] If it were
not thought of as existing, it could not be thought at all.

Moreover, is existence a predicate? Even if it is not would
it necessarily follow that specifications of existence are also
not predicates. The Proslogion does not use bare existence as a
predicate but suggests that reality, necessity, and independence
of existence are predicates of existence, that existence in re
can be distinguished from existence in intellectu, necessary from
contingent existence, and so forth. Furthermore, it is possible
to presuppose divine existence in a nonreal mode, and then argue
that an analysis of this being shows it to possess necessary
existence. Shaffer goes so far as to fault Kant with misrepre-
sentation of predication.[112] Existential propositions are always
synthetic. As synthetic propositions are those which add to the
concept of the subject a predicate which has not been thought in
it, 'exists' must be a predicate as it adds to the concept of
the subject. It is a real predicate.[113]

Though Shaffer may be mistaken, one must question that existence has nothing to do with the nature of a thing as expressed in predicates. Perhaps something is added when we say a thing exists. Kant's example of the hundred thalers is ambiguous. The concept of the hundred thalers is the same whether they do or do not exist only after they do, in fact, exist. Would a purely imaginary monetary unit be deposited in a real or a possible bank account?

It should be noted, however, that there is an opening, for a possible reformulation of Anselm's argument within Kantian thought. However it would not lead to a demonstration but to a transcendental argument, one not occupied with objects but with the mode of our knowledge of objects insofar as it is possible a priori. In the Proslogion, God is also revealed as Supreme Good and ground of the moral order. If in the Ideal of Reason there are valid obligations which require the assumption that a Supreme Being exists to give them effect and confirmation, this would entail the obligation to accept God's existence. The indecisiveness of speculation would be obviated and duty would require an affirmative answer.[114] Although this reformulation would entail a displacement from the speculative to the practical order, the similarities between Kant and Anselm in moral theory reinforce our impression that the point merits further exploration.

In retrospect, it seems that in spite of the force and rigor of Kant's criticism it is less than definitive, especially as it is grounded on a constellation of presuppositions which the themselves open to doubt. Still, Kant's critique of the 'ontological' argument marks a crucial turn. His presence is evident in almost all modern and contemporary scholarship dealing with the argument. Although he did attempt to disprove a version the argument, Kant generated interest in the proof, an interest that would later extend to Anselm and medieval thought, opening horizons for speculation and scholarship.

1. (<u>Opera</u> <u>Omnia</u> I) <u>Gaunilonis</u> <u>Pro</u> <u>Insipiente</u> (8), 129, 20-25.

2. "Dubitanti utrum sit vel neganti quod sit aliqua talis natura, qua nihil maius cogitari possit, cum esse illam hinc dicitur primo probari quod ipse negans vel ambigens de illa iam habeat eam in intellectu, cum audiens illam dici id quod dicitur intelligit; deinde quia quod intelligit necesse est ut non in solo intellectu sed etiam in re sit, et hoc ita probatur quia maius est esse et in re quam in solo intellectu, et si illud in solo est intellectu, maius illo erit quidquid etiam in re fuerit, ac sic maius omnibus minus erit aliquo et non erit maius omnibus quod utique repugnat." <u>Ibid.</u>, (1) 125, 3-10.

3. <u>Idem.</u>   4. <u>Ibid.</u>, (2), 125, 14-17.

5. <u>Ibid.</u>, 125, 21-126, 1.   6. <u>Ibid.</u>, 126, 1-4.

7. <u>Ibid.</u>, 126, 8-11.   8. <u>Ibid.</u> (3), 126, 17-18.

9. <u>Ibid.</u>, 126, 23-25.

10. Ontologism is an ambiguous term - The <u>Postulatum</u> <u>ad</u> <u>Concilium</u> <u>Vaticanum</u> <u>de</u> <u>Ontologismo</u> condemned only 'a certain form' of ontologism viz., that which teaches that "the direct and immediate knowledge of God is natural to man". It is described in this document as an "immediate principle in the system of Malebranche and of his disciples up to Gioberti". For further details refer to E. Gilson, T. Langan, A. Mauer, <u>Recent</u> <u>Philosophy</u>: <u>Hegel</u> <u>to</u> <u>the</u> <u>Present</u> (New York: Random House, 1966), pp. 261-265.

11. <u>Gaunilonis</u> <u>Pro</u> <u>Insipiente</u>, (4), 127, 2-3.

12. <u>Ibid.</u>, 127, 10-21.   13. <u>Idem.</u>

14. <u>Ibid.</u>, (5) 127, 28-128, 2.   15. <u>Idem.</u>

16. <u>Ibid.</u>, 128, 4-13.   17. <u>Idem.</u>

18. <u>Idem.</u>   19. <u>Idem.</u>, (6), 128, 14-32.

20. "Quapropter certissimo primitus aliquo probandum est argumento aliquam superiorem, hoc est maiorem ac meliorem

omnium quae sunt esse naturam, ut ex hoc alia iam possimus omnia comprobare, quibus necesse est illud quod maius ac melius est omnibus non carere". Ibid., (7), 129, 7-10.

21. Ibid., 129, 10-16.   22. Idem.

23. Pro Insipiente, (2), 125, 21-126, 1.

24. Responsio Editoria, (1), 130, 12-18.

25. Idem.

26. Ibid., 131, 1-2. "Si ergo cogitari potest esse, ex nec-
    essitate est". Ibid., 131, 5, (9) 138, 23-27.

27. Ibid., 131, 18-132, 2.

28. Ibid., (4), 134, 2-6; also (3) 133, 15-20; (1) 131, 29-132,
    2, et al.

29. Ibid., (1) 131, 6-11.   30. Ibid., 130, 20-131, 5.

31. Ibid., 131, 18-132, 2.   32. Ibid., 132, 3-5.

33. Ibid., (2), 132, 11-20.   34. Ibid., 132, 23-30.

35. Ibid., (8) 137, 14-18.   36. Ibid., (6), 136, 4-8.

37. Idem.   38. Ibid., (9), 138, 4-6.

39. Ibid., 138, 6-18.

40. But yet the distinguishing characteristic of God is that He
    cannot be thought of as not existing. "Sic igitur et
    proprium est deo non posse cogitari non esse." Ibid., (4),
    134, 16-17.

41. Ibid., (9), 138, 23-27.

42. "Nam et si nulla quae sunt possint intelligi non esse, omnia
    tamen possunt cogitari non esse, praeter id quod summe est."
    Ibid., (4) 133, 30-134, 2. Also Ibid., 133, 21-26; 134,
    16-17.

43. Ibid., 134, 2-6.   44. Ibid., (6), 136,10-21.

45. "Non enim idem valet quod dicitur 'maius omnibus' et 'quo
    maius cogitari nequit', ad probandum quia est in re quod
    dicitur." Ibid., (5), 134, 27-28; also Ibid., 134, 29-135,
    7.

46. Ibid., 135, 14-16.   47. Ibid., 135, 28-31.

48. Ibid., (10), 138, 28-30.

49. Jean Chatillon, "De Guillaume d'Auxerre à Saint Thomas d'Aquin. L'argument de saint Anselme chez les premiers scolastiques du XXIIe siecle," Spicilegium Beccense, p. 218.

50. Summa Theol. I, q. 2, a. 1.

51. Idem.

52. "Sed quia nos non scimus de Deo quid est, non est nobis per se nota: sed indiget demonstrari per ea quae sunt magis nota quoad nos, et minus nota quoad naturam scilicet per effectus." Idem.

53. Idem.   54. Idem.

55. Ibid., I, q. 2, a. 2.   56. Ibid., I, q. 2, a. 1.

57. Ibid., I, q. 93, a. 6.   58. Ibid., I, q. 93, a. 4.

59. Ibid., I, q. 93, a. 8.   60. Idem.

61. Ibid., I, q. 12, a. 12.

62. Jacques Maritain, Distinguer pour unir, ou Les degrés du savoir, trans. by G. P. Phelan, The Degrees of Knowledge (New York: Charles Scribner's Sons, 1959), p. 284.

63. Ibid., p. 278.

64. Opus Oxon., I, d. 2, n. 31. Latin-English text, edited and translated by Allan Wolter in Duns Scotus: Philosophical Writings (Toronto: Nelson, 1962), esp. pp. 73-76. Also Arthur Hyman and James J. Walsh, Philosophy in the Middle Ages: The Christian, Islamic, and Jewish Traditions (New York: Harper & Row, 1967), pp. 555-604; especially pp. 570-572.

65. Idem.   66. Idem.

67. Histoire de la philosophie: L'Antiquite et le Moyen Age, III: Le Moyen Age et le Renaissance (Paris: P.U.F., 1931), translated W. Baskin, The Middle Ages and the Renaissance (Chicago: University of Chicago Press (Phoenix), 1967), pp. 184-187.

68. Efrem Bettoni, <u>Duns Scotus</u>: <u>The Basic Principles of His Philosophy</u> (Washington: The Catholic University of America Press, 1961), p. 136.

69. <u>The Philosophical Works of Descartes</u>, ed. Haldane and Ross (London: Cambridge University Press, 1967), Vol. II, p. 45.

70. <u>Ibid</u>., p. 109. An interesting analysis is given by Gueroult, <u>Nouvelles Réflexions sur la Preuve Ontologique de Descartes</u> (Paris: J. Vrin, 1955), p. 72ff.

71. See Gueroult, <u>op</u>. <u>cit</u>., p. 29ff.; p. 56.

72. <u>Philosophical Works</u>, II, p. 107.

73. <u>Ibid</u>., p. 110.

74. <u>Ibid</u>., p. 118.

75. <u>Identität und Differenz</u> (Pfallingen: Neske, 1957), p. 20, cited by W. Richardson, "Heidegger and God and Professor Jonas"in <u>Thought</u>, Vol. XL, No. 156 (March '65), p. 29.

76. <u>Philosophical Works</u>, II, p. 94.

77. <u>Idem</u>.

78. Letter to Clerselier, <u>Ibid</u>., p. 129.

79. <u>Philosophical Works</u>, I, p. 166. This does not mean that we can comprehend all that is contained in the idea of God, but that which is comprehended is clear and distinct. The priority of the notion of God over the notion of myself is a <u>logical</u> priority; in the discovery of the <u>cogito</u> I discover myself as imperfect. The perfect is then the necessary condition, the presupposition, for the concept of myself.

80. <u>Ibid</u>., II, p. 34; p. 55, et al.

81. <u>Ibid</u>., p. 13.

82. <u>Ibid</u>., p. 12; 36; pp. 67-68.

83. <u>Ibid</u>., pp. 220-221.　　　　84. <u>Ibid</u>., p. 38.

85. <u>Ibid</u>., p. 17.　　　　　　　86. <u>Ibid</u>., p. 216.

87. <u>Ibid</u>., p. 108.　　　　　　　88. <u>Ibid</u>., p. 21.

89. Kant's <u>Critique</u> of <u>Pure</u> <u>Reason</u>, trans. by Norman Kemp-Smith (New York: St. Martin's Press, 1961), A591, B619.

90. <u>Idem</u>.; Cosmological Proof, A607, B635; Physico-Theological Proof, A629, B657.

91. <u>Ibid</u>., A592, B620.   92. <u>Ibid</u>., A593, B621.

93. <u>Ibid</u>., A596, B624.   94. <u>Ibid</u>., p. 503, note a.

95. <u>Ibid</u>., A597, B625.   96. <u>Ibid</u>., A599, B627.

97. <u>Ibid</u>., A600, B628.   98. <u>Ibid</u>., A601, B629.

99. <u>Ibid</u>., A602, B630.   100. <u>Ibid</u>., A604, B632.

101. <u>Ibid</u>., A568, B596; A569, B597.   102. <u>Ibid</u>., A569, B597.

103. <u>Ibid</u>., A571, B599.   104. <u>Idem</u>.

105. <u>Ibid</u>., A574, B602.   106. <u>Ibid</u>., p. 495, note a.

107. <u>Ibid</u>., A580, B608.   108. <u>Ibid</u>., A582, B610.

109. <u>Ibid</u>., A584, B612.

110. A. Koyré, <u>L'idée</u> de <u>Dieu</u> dans <u>la</u> philosophie de <u>S</u>. <u>Anselme</u> (Paris, 1923), pp. 231-234.

111. Malcolm, <u>op</u>. <u>cit</u>., p . 312ff.

112. Jerome Shaffer, 'Existence, Predication, and the Ontological Argument', in <u>The</u> <u>Many-faced</u> <u>Argument</u>, p. 228ff.

113. <u>Ibid</u>., pp. 228-230. There is something decidedly odd in stating, as does Hopkins, that "one real house may be better than another; but real houses are neither better nor worse than imagined ones." <u>A</u> <u>Companion</u> to the <u>Study</u> of <u>St</u>. <u>Anselm</u>, p. 73.

114. <u>Critique</u> of <u>Pure</u> <u>Reason</u>, A589, B617.

CHAPTER VII

CONTEMPORARY RESTATEMENTS

Allshouse

Under the presiding spirit of William James, Merle Allshouse has written a novel interpretation of the _Proslogion_ argument which views Anselm as a 'philosopher-theologian' of radical empiricism.[1] Familiar with contemporary Anselmian literature, Allshouse stops at many ports of call. The moderns are not neglected and though the medievals are practically excluded, it may well be that the scope of the work justifies their exclusion. Allshouse pretends to give a full interpretation, one that handles all dimensions of the _Proslogion_,[2] a re-examination which will endeavour to understand the argument as an organic whole.[3] He proposes a return to Anselm by providing "a new examination of the role of the affections and their relation to the process of concept formation."[4] This 'new interpretation' is indebted to Van der Leeuw,[5] Ushenko's field theory of meaning (the 'adequate schema' for understanding existential predication in the _Proslogion_[6]), James,[7] and many others including Santayana, Heidegger, Husserl, Northrop, Hartt, and Ingarden. In spite of this impressive catalogue, Allshouse insists that his interpretation is not mere patchwork.

This re-examination is based primarily on an extensive appraisal of the role of the affections within the structure of the _Proslogion_, stressing despair and joy. The argument, in Allshouse opinion, reflects two lives the "life of logic" and the "life of the affections" which is to say, conceptualization and subjective experience, actually two aspects of one unitary life.[8] Summarizing the task to be accomplished in the language of Ushenko's field theory of meaning, he indicates that it is (1) to show that there is an objective experience or inward vector which provides the initial phase of the argument; (2) to show how an examination of this initial experience produces a form of mental activity (outward vector) which is objectified in the language 'that-than-which-a-greater-cannot-be-thought'; (3) to show that the adequacy of the argument is judged by the degree to which the formulation of the second phrase 'illumines' and 'intensifies' the empirical experience of the first phase.[9]

The privileged affections of despair and joy[10] act as op-

posite poles of the Proslogion argument with the rational dialectic of <u>Proslogion</u> II-III, constituting a hermeneutical bridge
which mediates between them.[11] The argument has three phases or
moments, the pre-cognitive, the cognitive, and the post-cognitive.
This latter phase, reflected in the joy of the last chapter, is
the argument's principle of verification: "the post-cognitive
experience of joy is then the verification that Anselm has been
raised up, which, in turn, makes the conceptual phase adequate to
the pre-cognitive demand".[12] The <u>Proslogion</u>, has an 'affectional
structure' which initiates a movement which takes despair as its
point of departure, manifests itself in conceptualization, and
reaches out successfully to joy. Although joy is the index of
truth it is discovered only after a confrontation with despair.[13]

      God, according to Allshouse, arises within a context of
despair and anguish, a God who functions as "the very process of
deliverance from the situation so clearly described in the preface and the first chapter".[14] Reality is discovered by means of
the affections of fear and dread, 'affective qualities' encountered in the <u>Lebenswelt</u>. It is through the phenomenological
analysis of the range of human affections that direct verification procedures can be found.[15] Despair bears within itself the
hope for recovery. It points to that joy which has yet to be
attained. Whitehead's term <u>prehension</u> is used by Allshouse to
describe this intense, rich, form of experience, an "engagement
of the affections".[16] The outgrowth, then, of this prehending
experience of despair and anguish is the <u>Proslogion</u> II description of God.

      According to Allshouse it possesses a 'vector force' which
engages the felt tension between contingent and non-contingent,
forcing the mind to travel beyond the limit of static concepts.
The description, elaborated under the vector force of the experience of anguish and finitude,[17] presupposes that thinking is a
temporal act and that "the mind can be thrust forward in constant
attempting to conceive of a being greater than that conceived in
the previous concept at the previous moment".[18] Strictly speaking, 'a-being-than-which-nothing-greater-can-be-conceived' does
not describe God but the felt tension between contingent and non-
contingent.[19]

      The concept of existence arises from the <u>Lebenswelt</u>, the
world as encountered in everyday experience, Husserl's pre-predi-
cative experience. Anselm experiences, 'feels', the force of the
inward vector (the experienced tension) and the inadequacy of the
outward vector (the description of God) to balance this tension.
As the description is experienced to be inadequate it must, somehow, set straight and the imbalance between inward and outward
vectors overcome. We then have a further refining of the prehending process. God can be thought of as 'a-being-than-which-

nothing-greater-can-be-conceived' without his reality being exhausted in thought.[20] He is indicated by this description as is the target by the archer. The believer has less than an actual concept of God in his primitive notion of 'a-being-than-which-nothing-greater-can-be-conceived'.

As the quest for God is grounded in the Lebenswelt and His reality cannot be exhausted in cognition, it follows that the proposition 'God exists' is synthetic, not analytic.[21] To have a concept, for Anselm as opposed to Kant, is an act of empirical experience.[22] This is why Kant's 'definitive' critique of the argument is irrelevant. In the present context "existence is more than a predicate in the narrow grammatical sense of a descriptive attribute".[23] Furthermore, 'exists' does not even refer directly to God but rather to the God-description. To say that 'A exists' is to say that A is a member of a web of relations of interaction or spatio-temporal connection with the totality of other things.[24] To say 'God exists' is to indicate that there is an empirically verifiable relation between the description of God and the 'attitude of worship'.[25]

If Proslogion II presents the description of God, Proslogion III presents what Allshouse considers as the 'ultimate definite description', 'a-being-than-which-nothing-greater-can-be-conceived-to-exist-such-that-it-cannot-even-be-conceived-not-to-exist'. He interprets this as a further conceptual support for the outward vector which begins to measure up to the force of the inward vector. Conceptualization begins to measure up to experience. Necessary existence provides the link connecting the 'ultimate definite description' and the 'confessional statement' of Proslogion XVIII.[26] It is the logical expression proportionate to the encounter of the numinous in worship. It is a sharper focusing of the outward vector of conceptual formulation so as to effect a balancing of the force of the inward vector.[27] Finally, God is viewed as not only the highest thing the human mind is able to conceive but as beyond conception itself.[28] To deny the existence of such a being would entail a contradiction as thought itself is dependent on such a being, "the ultimate component of all thought and the experiencing of thought itself".[29]

Despair is the 'alpha' of (pre-cognitive) experience and joy the 'omega' (post-cognitive experience). Joy is the principle of verification and index of truth. It is joy which completes the argument and testifies to the fact that understanding has taken place.[30] Joy, presently experienced, verifies the adequacy of the function of 'God'.[31] This is truly an empirical verification. If we should ask what precisely does it verify, Allshouse responds that it verifies "the adequacy of the description of God provided in the second phase",[32] the cognitive phrase which acts as hermeneutic bridge between the affections of despair and joy.

113

It is the God-description given in _Proslogion_ III which is verified, not really the object of faith itself.

This radical empiricist metamorphosis of Anselm's argument has the merit of proposing a full interpretation and attempts to view it as an organic whole. The infrastructure of the _Lebenswelt_ produces the experience of despair which, when scrutinized, elicits a conceptual response. The response (the description of _Proslogion_ II) is at first inadequate, but finally balances out (the description of _Proslogion_ III), achieving an equilibrium which is attested to by the affection of joy. Allshouse takes those aspects of the argument which had previously been ignored (the affections, the relation between affections and concept formation, its relation to the life-world), and structures an interpretation which is interesting if only because of the possibilities it brings to light.

Critique

However, Anselm's claim to have discovered '_unum argumentum_' would seem to be refuted if this interpretation were accepted. Allshouse believes that his analysis will lead us to conclude that the argument depends on the cosmological proof, that it possesses an _a posteriori_ ground.[33] Aside from there being no textual basis for this assumption, Allshouse's use of the _Lebenswelt_ in this respect is rather ill advised.[34] Despair and joy as encountered in the _Proslogion_ are not affections in the proper sense. In the Victorine tradition, which Anselm did much to shape, as in St. Benedict's _Rule_, _affectus_ connotes a savoring or relishing of divine reality. There is little doubt that the joy of _Proslogion_ XXV-XXVI is more than an emotion on a human level. As it is found only _in spe_ it can hardly act as the principle of verification except perhaps in the eschaton. It is not a present, empirical verification as this joy without measure is simply not being experienced. Though Allshouse is quite right in affirming that the argument has traditionally been given an over-conceptualized interpretation,[35] it is rather farfetched to transform Anselm into a radical empiricist.

Allshouse in effect, secularizes the _Proslogion_ argument and, in doing so, reduces its grand proportions. Instead of the vast scenario of man's quest for God, we encounter a merely interesting updating of the argument. In place of praying in thought we are presented with a transition from despair to joy interpreted as a process of liberation. Allshouse is weak at Fool-analysis as he believes that the aim of the argument is not to refute the Fool's assertion that there is no God.[36] Again, his suggestion regarding possible verification of the argument by a community of sensitive men[37] misses the point. Nevertheless, Allshouse should be commended for attempting a novel interpretation of the argument in the face of the many difficulties and accumulated prejudices of centuries. The emphasis on the role of the affections and concept formation should prevent future Anselmian interpretation from disregarding these factors.

Hartshorne

While Allshourse's interpretation gives the appearance of being a creation of the moment Charles Hartshorne's interpretation in _Anselm's Discovery_ gives a different impression. It seems to be the result of constant investigation, spanning the greater part of an academic life: "I now think that both the standard criticisms and the older defenses, including mine of forty years ago, are all seriously - even disgracefully, defective".[38] The leitmotif of Hartshorne's ' contemporary Anselm' is that the essence-existence dichotomy is incapable of handling the argument, that a third term, _actuality_, is required to fully comprehend the _Proslogion_ discovery. An essence exists if there is some concrete reality exemplifying it. Existence entails that an essence is concretized, actuality how,in what particular form, it is concretized.[39] Although actuality is contingent, existence is not, as it requires only the 'non-emptiness' of the appropriate class of actualities. Applying this to Anselm's description of God as 'aliquid-quo-maius-nihil-cogitari-potest', Hartshorne distinguishes between the abstract definition and the not necessarily abstract existence which is deducible from it.[40] The abstract idea is neutral with respect to the particular manner (concrete reality) in which it may be actualized: yet to exist is to be somehow actualized in a suitable concrete and contingent reality It follows that God's existence is necessary but how God is actualized is contingent. Divine existence itself means that the abstract essence ('the impossibility of a superior') is actualized in a suitable contingent concrete form.[41] In Hartshorne's opinion, Anselm's discovery consists in affirming that in God, existence and actuality are distinct.

Hartshorne postulates that God's necessity is displayed in every truth and in every fact so that "when we have such a completed logic or theory of the _a priori_, the _idea_ of God will be integral to it".[42] The existence of God should then be knowable from any fact or denial of any fact. Experience, adequately interpreted, should open the path to God as He is the 'universal subject' and 'universal object' of knowing.[43] Based on the Anselmian principle of the non-contingency of Divine Existence,[44] the _Proslogion_ argument may be formulated so that "to conceive divinity and know that we do so is logically equivalent to knowing

that divinity or God exists".[45] If God is conceivable He exists.
If not, the theist is obliged to lapse into silence or to enlarge
his procedure of investigation.

The individuality of God is conceived as a pure determinable
which must be somehow particularized and concretized, as that
individual whose definitive functions are strictly universal and
coextensive with modality itself "the equivalence of modal coex-
tensiveness with Unsurpassability."[46] God, or as Hartshorne
seems to prefer, 'Divinity', is the ultimate determinable, bound
to be embodied in some concrete, determinate, form.[47] As the
abstract necessity of Divinity is empty, its concrete particu-
larization represents true freedom. Analogous to a necessary
proposition, entailed in any and every proposition, a necessary
being may be defined as "that which is contained in any and every
thing, actual or possible".[48] If the argument proves anything at
all, it is that 'Greatness', when thought of, must be thought of
as somehow actualized or really existent.[49]

Hartshorne views Anselm as a classical theist, far too much
of a Platonist, following the Greek habit of glorying in mere
unity.[50] This prevented Anselm from concluding that though, in a
sense, God is simple, in another sense, He may have more parts
than any other being, that the exaltation of God in worship does not
place Him above all other things, but above all other individu-
als.[51] God may conceivably surpass Himself. Grounded on Leibniz'
proof demonstrating the impossibility of the greatest conceivable
quantity and its corollary(the greatest conceivable quality is
impossible without the greatest conceivable quantity), one should
conclude that attributes incapable of maximization must also be
found in God, "provided they are capable of a form which is self-
surpassable only, in which form they too describe God."[52] In
this way, the difficulties which grow out of making God a pure
Absolute (the God of Philosophy, the Hellenic God, insensitive
and unreceptive to the world) is transcended.

Hartshorne admits that Kant's critique of the Proslogion II
argument is valid. Existence is taken to be a predicate. It is
also vulnerable to the objections of Findlay.[53] It should be
discarded in favor of the 'strong form' of the demonstration
given in the third chapter.[54] Anselm is here dealing with a unique and superior species of existence, necessary existence: emulating Philo, Hartshorne calls it 'existence-through-self' and
'existence-according-to-essence'. With respect to 'Supreme Greatness', conceivable non-existence must be ruled out a priori.
Proslogion III and the Reply present an acceptable proof, based
on conceptions of modal logic, dealing with two kinds of existence, contingent and necessary, instead of existence versus non-
existence or subjective versus objective existence as in the
second chapter.[55]

116

The 'common answer', that the premise of the Proslogion is
derived from faith, is rejected by Hartshorne as the proof would
then be fruitless except to those to whom it is already superfluous.[56] However, if believers would understand their faith
they would be the only ones to do so: only they would understand
the meaning of belief in God. Since a negative answer to the
question 'Does Divinity exist? is self-contradictory, to reject
an affirmative answer is to reject the question itself.[57] Even
the Fool thinks he knows the meaning of the word. God is such
that 'none-greater-can-be-conceived', greater signifying superior,
more excellent, more worthy of admiration and respect.[58] It is
the function of worship which requires the unqualified exaltation
of God beyond all possible rivalry. This 'neo-classical' interpretation endeavours to support Anselm's argument without mini-
mizing the strength and validity of the objections lodged against
it.

As God's existence is the essential element to all existence,
He cannot possibly be unreal. Divine individuality or existence
is contained in every individual "affirmed when it is affirmed
and denied when it is denied".[59] It alone enjoys total compos-
sibility as it is compatible with any and all other existences.
God could have any predicate or compossible set of predicates
whatsoever.[60] Because of this any evidence for God's existence
will be wholly intellectual and spiritual, not sensory.[61]

Critique

Perhaps the most unsettling aspect of Anselm's Discovery is
its somewhat diffuse presentation. Hartshorne does not maintain
a sustained level of thought but has a penchant for wandering off
course. In spite of his many 'discoveries', Hartshorne's rein-
terpretation of the Proslogion argument is nebulous, and one is
left with the feeling that the original formulation is more satisfactory. Furthermore, Hartshorne bases his interpretation on
a peculiar conception of religious belief. His contention that
the central religious belief must possess necessary truth is not
beyond question. Does the believer want to understand the meaning of belief in God, or simply of God exists and if so, what can
be known about Him. Does a believer really wants to discover a
theory of the a priori? Hartshorne's notion of God - a 'Christian' God - with both surpassable and unsurpassable aspects, simple and composed of parts, presents serious difficulties. It
might be objected that a measureable God would be reduced to the
status of an intramundane being, subject to norms external to
Himself. If a God unsurpassable to Himself would be insensitive
and unreceptive to the world, wouldn't Hartshorne's God run the
risk of being, at least in some aspect, identified with the

world? Panentheism is a legitimate option but not one that is peculiar to Christianity.

Hartshorne might also be faulted for identifying 'quo-maius-cogitari-nequit' with greatest, supreme greatness, greatness, perfect, and unsurpassability. Although he is attempting more than an interpretation of Anselm's argument and fidelity to the text is not essential, it is none the less rash to discard Anselm's repeated warnings that 'quo-maius-cogitari-nequit' is the privileged God-description and the point of departure for the argument. Furthermore, Hartshorne's dismissal of experience as a pertinent factor in the argument might be faulted, as it does seem to have some place in the argument albeit in a subordinate role.

The conception of God as universal subject and universal object of knowledge as well as his analogy between a necessary proposition and a necessary being provide valuable suggestions regarding Anselm's possible incorporation into contemporary philosophy. It well may be an updating, an authentic echo, of Anselm's principle of rectitude. A similar transition from the truth of a proposition to God as Supreme Truth is made by Anselm in the Monologion,[62] and is found again, more than a decade later, in the De Veritate, following a section which begins with the assertion "summam autem veritatem non negabis rectitudinem esse".[63] As Supreme Rectitude, God grounds the existential, cognitive, and moral orders. Perhaps the 'rootedness' of all orders could provide the point of departure for a proof, contemporary in temper, which would be more than a variation on the usual textbook arguments. Anselm's theory of propositional truth would certainly be one of the possible routes to follow. Hartshorne provides us with a valuable but as yet unfinished chart for future exploration.

Allshouse and Hartshorne are not the only ones to present reformulations of the Proslogion argument. Both Zubiri's proof through 'religación' and Duméry's 'fourth reduction' are novel proofs, which have the Proslogion as their spiritual home. Far less innovative but valuable studies have been written by many lovers of Anselm, Malcolm and Moreau among them. Even Findlay's argument for the 'non-existence' of God has Anselmic roots and is a somewhat reluctant tribute to the argument. In spite of being very solidly anchored in a particular historical era and culture the argument has always transcended its horizon and demanded an adequate formulation in the vocabulary of the times. Contemporary philosophy is not immune to this exigency. Whether it has proven adequate to the task is another question indeed.

NOTES

1. M.F. Allshouse, _An_ _Evaluation_ _of_ _Anselm's_ _Ontological_ _Argu-ment_, unpublished Ph.D. dissertation (Ann Arbor: University Microfilms), No. 66-4877, II. _Ibid._, p. 247.

2. _Ibid._, 6.

3. This organic character of the argument can be understood, only if by 'understanding' we mean "an experienced process of living with phenomena with sufficient patience and empathy to find structure", 15.

4. _Ibid._, 167-168; 210.

5. Van der Leeuw's method provides him "with an adequate framework for understanding Anselm". (I).

6. _Ibid._, 19.   7. _Ibid._, 213f.

8. _Ibid._, 76; 243.   9. _Ibid._, 238.

10. Despair is a unique affection indeed. It is "more like the despair of a lover who cannot find an adequate mode of expression for the beloved." (221). It should not be confused with the "emotion of one who sees existence dropping off into sheer non-being." (_Ibid._)

11. _Ibid._, 20.   12. _Ibid._, 237, 59.

13. _Ibid._, 230.   14. _Ibid._, 40.

15. _Ibid._, 216.   16. _Ibid._, 241.

17. _Ibid._, 29ff.   18. _Ibid._, 113.

19. 'God', for Allshouse, is a functional proper name. 'God' functions as "the very process of deliverance" from the initial despair and anguish (46). It will be judged as more or less adequate by "the function it performed in moving the mind towards the infinite as the ultimate ontological and logical support of the finite" (48). If it exercises this function then it may be pronounced adequate. This functional proper name is not God, though it can point in His direction.

20. _Ibid._, 84.   21. _Ibid._, 88.

119

22. Ibid., 87.

23. Ibid., 64. Allshouse states "...existence is a predicate in the logical sense of that which is affirmed or denied of a subject, although existence is not a predicate in the narrow grammatical sense of a descriptive attribute...to say then that 'God exists' can be meaningful if we have given some descriptive characteristics to 'God'. We may then predicate existence not as an additional characteristic, but as a signal that there is an inward vector which invites increasing specification through description."

24. Ibid., 94f.   25. Ibid., 29.

26. Ibid., 122.   27. Ibid., 81.

28. Ibid., 98-99.   29. Ibid., 102.

30. Ibid., 17.   31. Ibid., 46.

32. Ibid., 346f.

33. Allshouse, op. cit., 15: 29. et al.

34. Refer to Aron Gurvitsch, The Problem of Existence: Studies in Phenomenology and Psychology (Evanston: Northwestern University Press, 1966) 120-121; also 418-428.

35. Allshouse, op. cit., 211ff.

36. Ibid., 95.   37. Ibid., 216.

38. Anselm's Discovery: A Re-examination of the Ontological Proof for the Existence of God,(LaSalle: Open Court, 1962), p. ix.

39. Ibid., p. x.   40. Ibid., p. 38.

41. Id.   42. Ibid., p. 44.

43. Ibid., p. 46.

44. Ibid., p. 52. This 'true' Anselmian principle is found in Proslogion III. A 'false' Anselmian principle is encountered in the second chapter viz., 'to exist is better than not to exist' (p. 88). The whole second chapter is, in Hartshorne's opinion, to be decried "to have prefaced the great third by his inferior second chapter was indeed a sad blunder of Anselm's (p. 90). It is a poor presentation of the case as "contingency is a weakness in a much clearer sense than mere non-existence" (p. 102). In taking non-existence ('unless a

thing exists there are no properties of the thing') we appear
to be committing the 'homological fallacy', making the universal an instance of itself. Taking "contingency as the
defect, we can then compare in thought a necessarily-existing
and a contingently-existing thing, and decide which must be
greater" (p. 102).

45. Ibid., p. 53.   46. Ibid., p. 58.

47. Ibid., p. 4; 19.   48. Ibid., p. 80.

49. Ibid., p. 83.   50. Ibid., p. 27.

51. Ibid., pp. 28-29.   52. Ibid., p. 32.

53. Findlay's critique is found in his "Can God's Existence be
    Disproved" in Mind, 57 (1948), pp. 176-183. In brief, his
    argument is as follows: Anselm is right in holding that God
    must be supposed to exist necessarily. A being worthy of
    worship could not have contingent existence; "it must be
    conceived as inescapable and necessary, whether for thought
    or reality" and possess "unsurpassable supremacy, tower
    infinitely above all other objects". But these requirements
    lead to a far different conclusion. Modern logic shows that
    no existence can be necessary, that concrete or actual exist-
    ence cannot follow from a predicate or abstract definition.
    Hence, we arrive at God's necessary non-existence. When this
    article was published in Findlay's Language, Mind, and Value
    (London: Allen and Unwin, 1963), the author prefaced it with
    the following words: "I still think it makes a valid point;
    that if it is possible, in some logical and not merely epis-
    temological sense, that there is no God, then God's existence
    is not merely doubtful but impossible, since nothing capable
    of non-existence could be a God at all... Professor Hartshorne
    has, however, convinced me that my argument permits a ready
    inversion, and that one can very well argue that if God's
    existence is in any way possible, then it is also certain and
    necessary that God exists, a position which should give some
    comfort to the shade of Anselm...... The notion of God, like
    the notion of the class of all classes not the members of
    themselves, has plainly unique logical properties, and I do
    not now think that my article finally decided how we should
    cope with such uniqueness".

54. Hartshorne, op. cit., p. 33.   55. Ibid., p. 16.

56. Ibid., p. 22.   57. Ibid., p. 25.

58. Ibid.,pp. 25-26.   59. Ibid., p. 114.

60. Ibid., p. 123. 61. Ibid., p. 104.

62. Monologion, 18; 33, 9-23.

63. De Veritate, 10; (Opera I), 190, 13-32.

CHAPTER VIII

CONTEMPORARY CRITICISM

As stated, the purpose of this study is to present a comprehensive introduction to Anselm's Proslogion argument, not to trace out a genealogy of 'ontological arguments' from Anselm's time to the present. Precisely because of this, Hartshorne and Allshouse have been accorded privileged status, being attempts to return to the source and interrogate the text itself. Whatever the difficulties found in their interpretations does not diminish the courage displayed in their effort to disengage the argument from the accretions which have encumbered it so as to present it in a contemporary framework. It must be remembered that even the most serious of the objections which have been covered, Aquinas and Kant, as well as Descartes' formulation, have been studied primarily in an archeological spirit: to rescue the Proslogion argument from the ravages of time, custom, and academic ossification. Because of this priority, though many contemporary studies on the argument have been cited, they have been used rather sparingly, most often to elucidate a point, to add contour and shading to an attempted hermeneutic. It does not pretend to scratch the surface of 'ontological' argument literature, much of which is valuable, not only because of its own merits, but insofar as Proslogion interpretation is concerned. These studies range from the historical to the systematic, from those which deal directly with Anselm and the Proslogion to those endless disputations in which the argument has been disfigured beyond recognition. The more prominent of these studies as well as others should be cited anew, precisely at those points relevant to Proslogion interpretation. To omit them would be a disservice to Anselm and the argument, though to enter into minute detail and exhaustive analysis would certainly lie beyond the limits of the present study.

Historical Studies

Perhaps the most important historical work of the past decade or so is Joseph Moreau's Pour ou contre l'insensé? Essai sur la preuve Anselmienne.[1] He distinguishes between the Monologion and the Proslogion by the Platonic distinction between diánoia and noesis.[2] Though ingenious, this is only a fairly safe analogy which tends to promote a somewhat distorted perspective which

123

affects his interpretation. However, when he states that the
argument "is not a discourse, a concatenation of reasons but an
'élévation', an effort of the spirit to attain contemplation, to
obtain understanding of that which is believed",[3] one can agree
wholeheartedly. Moreau's emphasis on the importance of 'Platonic'
interiority, citing texts from the Theatetus, Sophist, and the
Philebus,[4] is refreshing and instructive. Furthermore, his
insistence that 'quo-maius-cogitari-nequit' is not an object
exterior to its concept, but an absolute being which transcends
it, that the ontological argument does not conclude from an idea
to the reality of its object, but ascends from the idea to the
absolute principle of being and thought,[5] presents valuable notions which can be accepted.

Moreau understands that Anselm's faith (quaerens intellectum)
is not curiosity, searching for reasons to confirm belief. Nor
is it a confirmation through discursive reason (faculté dianoe-
tic), but rather a quest for intuitive vision, the contact of the
nous with truth.[6] This élévation begins with obscure but ineffable presence of God in our soul".[7] The existence of God is affirmed not as the consequence of implication grounded on the concept of 'quo-maius-cogitari-nequit' but on the presence in human
thought of eternal and necessary truth.[8]

This brings to mind several interpretations given under the
guiding spirit of Hegel,[9] but Moreau's inspiration is basically
Platonic with a relatively minor admixture of Neo-Platonism.
However, his insight into the Proslogion argument is somewhat
obscured by his apparent neglect of the Christian character of
Anselm's thought. The notion of the argument as a sort of revelation naturelle[10] is suspect from a Christian point of view and
untenable within the context of Anselm's thought. The comparison
between the Monologion (diánoia), and the Proslogion (noesis) is
barely admissible as the difference between Hellenic theoria and
Christian contemplatio is not taken into consideration. There
seems to be a parallel tendency to obviate the distance between
the description of God and God Himself, between an event within
consciousness and the its very root and source, which would lead
to a sort of ontologism. Although Moreau states that the argument "aspire à l'illumination", he includes more than mere aspiration within the limits of the Proslogion, while understanding
illumination as an intellectual noesis, rather different from
the state described by Anselm in the last two chapters of the
Proslogion.

In spite of the above objections, Moreau's small book is
decidedly a scholarly and valuable contribution to Anselmiana,
and suggests possibilities for further exploration. A second
work, by A. C. McGill, a rather extensive article,[11] provides a
knowledgeable summary and evaluation of recent discussions of the

argument, though the author's evaluation of the argument, given in six pages, is somewhat ingenuous. None the less, McGill recognizes the complexity of the argument, the insufficiency of the 'standard interpretation', which sees the whole operation as moving exclusively on the level of ideas,[12] and emphasizes the unity between Proslogion II and III,[13] the latter viewed as a refinement or development of the former.[14] However, it is as a critic that McGill is at his best.

Firstly, McGill points to the difficulties endemic to usual interpretations of the argument. The rationalistic interpretations run up against Anselm's insistence on the primacy of faith over reason,[15] while the Anselm as believer hypotheses depend on the hazardous denial of any trace of rationalism. Following André Hayen, McGill suggests that Anselm's 'truly universal reasoning' is meant not only delight the monks at Bec and Christians, but to engage the thinking of all men.[16] At this point, McGill does a good job of straddling the fence, his own opinion is suggested rather than stated outright.

According to McGill, all interpretations of the argument can be subsumed under six categories, (1) Realistic Idea; (2) Noetic Datum; (3) Limit to Conceiving; (4) Reflexive Discovery; (5) Revealed Rule for Thought and (6) Monologion grounded. In the first, the Realistic interpretation - McGill cites Kolping[17] - Anselm is viewed as beginning with a direct cognition of God's reality. Here, the power of the argument does not depend on the validity of its logic but on the initial awareness (of God) which it elaborates.[18] The idea of God already stands in the domain of the real and is an apprehension of the real. This interpretation, according to McGill, has the advantage of seeing the argument as the analysis of something certain, not the verification of something uncertain, "a recognition of God in His presence".[19] Its grave defect is that it flies in the face of the evidence. Anselm makes many strictures against such direct awareness.[20] It might be added the Proslogion XV, in which God is declared to surpass human thought, would also militate against this interpretation.

The second group, following Dom Beda Adlhoch and Gilson,[21] reads Anselm in the light of Descartes' Third Meditation. God is proposed to be the cause of either the idea (of God) or of the logical necessity which the mind discovers in this idea: "the argument is actually cosmological".[22] But these interpretations run up against the fact that Anselm did not "construe the intellectual life in the Cartesian manner, as data inside the mind which are somehow 'caused' by realities which are outside".[23] Rather, Anselm views the intellectual life as man's active openness towards real entities through understanding and towards possible entities through conceiving.[24] McGill is acute in his observations though the problem requires additional elaboration.

The third category of interpreters considers the divine not as the cause of a datum in the mind, but rather as a limit of a certain mental operation.[25] Conceiving (knowing) is really not completely free. The human mind can only devise that which is in some way objectively possible. The connection between conceiving and the possible provides the key to the argument: "the proof begins, not with an idea, but with a noetic limit, imposed by, and therefore indicative of, reality itself".[26] The logic of the argument demonstrates that the initial limit by which the mind is unable to conceive of anything greater than God entials other limits: not being able to affirm (Proslogion I) or even conceive of (Proslogion II) God's nonexistence. The novelty of Anselm's discovery resides in postulating God as the Lord and limit of all possibility.[27] Imagination is as much subject to God as is objective reason. This interpretation has the merit of placing the argument within the context of the Christian doctrine of creation and rejecting the 'pagan' belief--attributed by McGill to Gaunilo--that the divine can be taken seriously only if it dwells within the sphere of the actual.[28] Yet it seems to run counter to Anselm's belief that the argument is valid by itself alone, and presupposes an exegesis not explicitly authorized by the text.[29]

The fourth (Reflexive Discovery) and fifth (Revealed Rule for Thought) interpretations have already been mentioned in passing, the first that of Forest, and second that of Barth.[30] Forest stipulates that once the idea of God is seen to be in the mind there follows the recognition that God Himself is present there, activating it to think this idea.[31] Reflexive knowledge comprises that which the mind learns about itself while in the process of thinking about objects. It accompanies 'projective thought'.[32] The Fool attempts to think God by thinking 'something-than-which-nothing-greater-can-be-thought'. This very effort discloses the existence of God in Himself "within and behind this very mental effort."[33] The difficulty encountered here is that it appears to require the identity of the idea of God and God Himself, quite different from Anselm's belief in the immense gulf between creative and created reality.[34] Insofar as Barth is concerned, enough has already been said. McGill's principal objection is that Barth bases the power of the argument wholly upon the authority of God an authority to which Anselm himself did not find it necessary to have recourse.[35]

As McGill indicates, it was standard practice for nineteenth-century historians to base the argument on the proofs offered in the Monologion.[36] The main support for this view comes from the Responsio in which Anselm repeats arguments he had previously developed in the Monologion. The difficulty here is that this openly contradicts Anselm's stated purpose in the preface of the Proslogion, attempting to escape a complex tangle of reasoning to find an argument which would require for its proof _nullo alio quam sibi solo_.[37] Furthermore, Anselm emphasizes that the words of the description have only to be heard and understood for the argument to be convincing. Nothing else is required.[38]

McGill indicates that all of these interpretations àre shaped by a common but unrecognizable principle, a principle so alien to Anselm "that no fully satisfactory interpretation can be achieved".[39] Anselm depends on the power of ordinary words and is convinced that hearing words is an event of genuine knowledge, "that words themselves have the power to initiate some kind of relation of understanding between the listening mind and reality".[40] Anselm follows Augustine in his confidence in the power of language, different from the modern interpretations of the argument which reject the principle that words can produce knowledge.[41] While for the moderns language is a 'mental epiphenomenon', a 'tool for subjectivity', for Anselm it might have been an immediate intuition or reflexive discovery or an encounter with revelation or a cosmological inference".[42] Following Heidegger, McGill suggests that perhaps words are the instruments of reality and do not express merely human ideas but reality in its state of unveiledness: "in every statement it is the subject matter--not the subjectivity of the author--which addresses man's thought."[43] This 'new' view of language may lead to a new approach to the argument.[44]

McGill's solution is anticlimactic. Though we are in his debt for opening a new avenue of _Proslogion_ interpretation, it is based, as McGill admits, on a return to St. Paul with a nod to Heidegger: faith proceedes from hearing. However, this avenue merits exploration and it is hoped that the sketchy outline presented will be filled in at some time in the future.

Systematic Studies

Of the many studies dedicated to the argument from a systematic point of view, some are valuable as suggestions or hints which can be incorporated into any interpretation. Aside from these there are studies which deserve less cavalier treatment and have generated discussion and debate. The principal difficulty we are faced with here is that only a few are inclined to take history seriously and delight in working with the bare logical bones of an 'ontological' argument which does not correspond to the _Proslogion_ text. Rowe accurately points out that the 'ontological' argument is a family of arguments, each of which beings with a concept of God and, by appealing only to _a priori_ principles, endeavours to establish that God actually exists.[45]

His own presentation, by the way, is not notable for its textual fidelity to Anselm, but certainly deserves mention. The 'key-idea' in the argument is that existence-in-reality is a great-making quality. A comparison between two things, one existing and the other not existing, concluding that the first is greater than the other, is not given. What the argument does is to take one thing, "pointing out that if it does not exist but might have existed, then it would have been a greater thing if it had existed."[46] Anselm's argument is a <u>reductio ad absurdum</u>: if we suppose that God does not exist it leads to an absurd result. But the argument has its Achilles' heel. In granting the premise that God is a possible being, more is granted than is intended as the notion of God logically cannot apply to some non-existent thing. It could apply only to a possible object which, in effect, does exist.[47] Even if Anselm's concept of God is coherent, and his principle that existence is a great-making quality true, one can conclude only that no non-existing thing can be Anselm's God.[48]

Richard Taylor makes an interesting contribution when he indicates that in spite of the standard objection (the illicit transition from the conceptual to the real order), all men are accustomed to doing this when it comes to denying the existence <u>in re</u> of certain things: "from one's clear understanding of what is meant by a plain four-sided figure, all of whose points are equidistant from the center, one can conclude with certainty that no such being exists in reality."[49] Shaffer and others, although they do not accept this defense, find the standard criticisms to be totally unconvincing.[50] Though Shaffer's notion of the argument is somewhat ingenuous and un-Anselmian (the 'ontological' argument purports to show that God must exist because the condition that He exists is a part of the definition of the kind of thing He is),[51] his attempt to apply the distinction between extension and intension to the argument is not without merit.

We cannot tell by the 'form' of an expression how it is being used.[52] The sentence 'God exists' may be used both tautologically and non-tautologically: it may be claimed that the term 'God' has extension, that it applies to some existent. None the less, the argument's only valid conclusion is an intensional statement about the meaning of the concept of God: "the <u>prima facie</u> plausibility of the Argument comes from the use of a sentence intensionally when the typical use of that sentence is extensional".[53] This is to say it conceals an illicit move from an intensional to an extensional statement. Something additional is needed to establish that the concept of God has extension, over and above its intensional features. An <u>a posteriori</u> argument is needed "to the effect that certain evidences make it reasonable to think that some actual existent answers to the concept."[54] And this is, adds Shaffer, just as religious men would want it.

God cannot be thought as exhausted in the concepts and propositions of a language game, as He affects the world and may possibly be experienced.[55]

Gilbert Ryle, in two brief articles, originally published in
Mind, launched an attack against the Neo-Hegelian interpretation
of the 'ontological' argument.[56] From his point of view, to
believe that a form of the 'ontological' argument is not only
valid, but presupposed by the best of philosophical argument,
that it has not been seriously criticized since Hegel, almost
merits tears.[57] This mistaken view(attributed to Collingwood)
attempts to dismiss one of the 'biggest advances in logic' made
since Aristotle: Hume's and Kant's discovery that particular matters of fact cannot be the implicates of general propositions,
and cannot be demonstrated from a priori premises.[58] Existence-
propositions are synthetic and never logically necessary. Ryle
considers it to be "rather shocking that there should exist a
large school of thought which treats as a well-established principle a doctrine which has been for a century and a half accused
of formal fallaciousness."[59] This objection in its standard
form is taken to task by Alston who concludes by presenting
sounder reasons for denying that 'exists' is a predicate.[60]

The standard argument against treating 'exists' as a predicate collapses, in Alston's opinion, once we realize that there
are different modes of existence: "once we stretch the notion of
place to include fiction, mythology, imagination and the real
world, it becomes very unclear what could be meant by the existence which could indifferently be exercised in these locales."[61]
As existence is not a genus, the argument may be reformulated in
a way which is impervious to the usual objections. Let us presuppose the existence of a perfect being in some 'nonreal mode'
where existence is obvious and then argue that an analysis of
this being demonstrates that it possesses real existence. Alston
accurately observes that this is the form of Anselm's argument,
and that the difference between Anselm and Descartes in this
regard has been too little remarked.[62] None the less, when we
predicate real existence of a perfect being we are seized with
'logical vertigo'[63]

Alston insists that we must recognize that the kind of existence which is posited will put limits on the sort of predication which can be made. An existential statement determines a
'logical framework' within which predications can be made: it is
a sort of license to make certain types of subject-predicate
statements and not others.[64] Unfortunately this license does not
cover Anselm's argument. The statement which Anselm claims to be
necessarily true is a statement about a being in the understanding. As such it exhibits the logical features of statements
based on a presupposition of mental existence.[65] To exist in

reality here is not an ordinary statement of real existence. It can have no implications with respect to the real world, except for the fact that Anselm is thinking a certain idea. Although it is possible to make a transition from one mode of existence to another, it is impossible to construe existential statements as predicative.[66] But certain possibilities are still open: "the demonstration that 'exists' is not a predicate does nothing to show that no existential statements are necessary".[67]

Alston's critique is based on his acceptance of the thought-reality dichotomy: "the dissection of what is in the understanding will never tell us what is in the real world, any more than analysis of my dreams will ever tell me which of their contents, if any, faithfully represent real objects".[68] This would be tantamount to lifting ourselves by our bootstraps, unlocking a door by staring at the lock, and so on. He seems to fear that if existence in one mode entailed existence in another, the barriers between the two would crumble.[69] But the dichotomy between reality and thought is itself a chancy point of departure.

Perhaps the most provocative systematic study is Norman Malcolm's, 'Anselm's Ontological Arguments'.[70] In brief, Malcolm contends that there are two 'ontological' arguments. The first, given in Proslogion II, is fallacious because it rests on the 'false doctrine' that existence is a perfection and therefore a real predicate.[71] Though it is erroneous and 'remarkably queer', Malcolm admits that he has not elaborated a rigorous refutation but is compelled to leave the matter at the more or less intuitive level of Kant's observation.[72] The second 'ontological' proof[73]- Anselm probably did not think of himself as offering two proofs - is given in Proslogion III. The argument does not maintain that existence is a perfection but rather that the logical impossibility of non-existence is a perfection. Necessary existence is a perfection.[74] The notion of either contingent existence or contingent non-existence cannot refer to God.[75] God's existence is either logically necessary or logically impossible. The only way of rejecting Anselm's claim at this point is to maintain that the concept of God as 'a-being-a-greater-than-which-cannot-be-conceived' is self-contradictory or nonsensical.

Although the two-argument hypothesis serves to clarify Proslogion III, it seems to interrupt the momentum of the argument. Anselm insists that it is important to posit the existence of 'something-than-which-nothing-greater-can-be-thought' in the mind as it provides the initial base for the argument. The third chapter builds on and completes the argument of Proslogion II. It is noteworthy that although his interpretation is marred by a piece of forced psychologizing,[76] Malcolm touches on the religious value of the argument: "it may help to remove some philosophical scruples which stand in the way of faith".[77] At a deeper level he suggests that the argument can be thoroughly understood only from the inside, by those with some inclination to partake in the religious form of life.[78]

One of the weaknesses of this approach is indicated by Paul Henle, who faults Malcolm with not providing his interpretation with a solid grounding, the Neo-Platonic identification of existence with reality and fullness of being.[79] Without 'metaphysical buttressing' of this sort the argument is weak. Henle believes Gaunilo would be on the right track in asking why the argument does not prove the existence of his 'perfect island', if Anselm were not implying that in accordance with Neo-Platonic principles a perfect island is a contradiction in terms.[80] He also picks up a rather unfortunate remark of Malcolm's - that God possesses necessary omnipotence[81] - to inquire what is the _differentia_ of this sort of omnipotence and "what can a being which has necessary omnipotence do which a being that merely has omnipotence cannot."[82]

Henle's major difficulty with the argument - or at least Malcolm's version - is not being able to make any sense out of necessary existence.[83] It seems to require belief in God to even pose the question regarding necessary existence. Henle does not think that the argument, even with Neo-Platonic buttressing,is really meant to demonstrate or convince, but to remind the Christian of his beliefs: to summarize them. It does not convert but clarifies the beliefs of the already converted. The only function of the 'ontological' argument--in Anselm as well as Descartes--is to 'summarize' and 'encapsulate' what preceeded it.[84]

The argument does have a didactic function, but to limit it in this way is clearly at odds with Anselm's goal which includes both demonstration and aspiration to contemplation. It is only a half truth to state--as does Henle--that reason is not the basis of faith but presupposes faith and exists for the clarification of faith.[85] Reason presupposes faith in the sense that by faith reason is reestablished in its proper domain but this in no way limits the function of reason to the clarification of faith. Nonetheless, given the acuity of his critique of Malcolm and his insights into the nature of the argument, one can only lament that an expanded study is not at hand.

Jasper Hopkins' _A Companion to the Study of St. Anselm_[86] provides an excellent introduction and commentary on the main Anselmian themes together with an extensive bibliography and translation of the 'philosophical fragments'.[87] This study is unique in its appreciation of Medieval and Classical sources as well as a solid grasp of Anselm's work. Hopkins' presentation is lucid and scholarly. The section on Truth and possibility[88] can be studied with benefit before engaging in _Proslogion_ interpretation. Unfortunately, the chapter dedicated to the 'ontological argument'[89] is not characteristic of the remainder of the book.

Instead of studying the _Proslogion_ argument on its own grounds with its peculiar theological, philosophical, and religious presuppositions, Hopkins engages in a running controversy with Malcolm whose interpretation of the argument, including the two argument hypothesis, he seems to equate with Anselm. Though it is far from outrageous to consider Malcolm as the ablest exponent of the _Proslogion_ argument, to do so while faulting him with ignoring the importance of possibility in Anselm's thought,[90] does detract from his interpretation. In any case, Malcolm shares Anselm's fate in sharing his convictions.[91] The argument, in stressing the dubious relationships between existence and conceivability makes "the mistake of inferring from a unique and self-consistent description something affirmative about matters of fact".[92] The objection is a serious, though one we have come to recognize as standard. From such a proficient Anselmian scholar one might have expected a more original approach.

Contemporary scholarship regarding the 'ontological' argument is unequal.[93] Dispassionate scholarship is to be found and much good work has been done on both historical and the systematic levels. The abundance of the literature on the argument is a tribute to Anselm and the _Proslogion_. Renewed interest in a theme which is scarcely in accord with contemporary taste confirms its status as a philosophical classic.

1. Joseph Moreau, _Pour ou contre l'insensé? Essai sur la preuve Anselmienne_ (Paris: Vrin, 1967).

2. _Ibid._, pp. 7-8.

3. _Ibid._, p. 8; 11.

4. _Ibid._, p. 17, note 35. The texts are _Theatetus_ 190a ff; _Sophist_, 263e ff; _Philebus_, 38e ff.

5. _Ibid._, p. 56. Also p. 73 ff.   6. _Ibid._, p. 8.

7. _Ibid._, p. 11.   8. _Ibid._, p. 57.

9. See Edward Caird, "Anselm's Argument for the Being of God", in the _Journal of Theological Studies_ I, 1 (October 1899), esp. pp. 31-35. R. G. Collingwood, _An Essay on Philosophical Method_ (Oxford: Clarendon Press, 1933), pp. 123-136; E. E. Harris, "Mr. Ryle and the Ontological Argument" in _Mind_, Vol. XLV, N.S., No. 180 (October, 1936), pp. 474-480.

10. Moreau, _op. cit._, p. 11.

11. Arthur C. McGill, "Recent Discussions of Anselm's argument", in _The Many-Faced Argument_, ed. John Hick and A. C. McGill (New York: The MacMillan Co., 1967), pp. 33-110.

12. _Ibid._, p. 34.   13. _Ibid._, p. 39.

14. _Ibid._, p. 42.   15. _Ibid._, p. 55.

16. _Ibid._, p. 63.

17. McGill, _op. cit._, pp. 71-29. Adolf Kolping, _Anselms Proslogion - Beweis der Existenz Gottes in Zusammenhang seines Spekulativen Programms_ (Bonn: Hanstein, 1939).

18. McGill, _op. cit._, pp. 71-72.   19. _Ibid._, p. 74.

20. _Ibid._, p. 78.

21. _Ibid._, pp. 79-83. Dom Beda Adlhoch, "Der Gottesbeweis des hl. Anselm", in _Philosophische Jahrbuch der Görres-Gesellschaft_ VIII (1895), pp. 52-69, 372-389; IX (1896), pp. 280-

287; x (1897), pp. 261-274, 394-416. Etienne Gilson, 'Sens Et Nature....', pp. 9 ff., 13 ff. McGill gives Gilson credit for elaborating a more subtle form of the argument: "Anselm, he contends, appeals to God's reality as the cause, not of the initial idea as such, but rather of the logical necessity which the mind discovers in analyzing the idea", p. 81. Gilson, of course, considers the argument fallacious: "where St. Anselm went wrong...was in failing to notice that the necessity of affirming God, instead of constituting in itself a deductive proof of His existence, is really no more than the basis for an induction." The Spirit of Mediaeval Philosophy (New York: Charles Scribner's Sons, 1936), p. 60.

22. Ibid., p. 79.   23. Ibid., p. 82.

24. Idem.

25. Ibid., pp. 83-89. McGill notes that "although no individual has developed this interpretation with consistent thoroughness, commentators often make fragmentary use of it", p. 83, note 169. He refers only to P. Michaud-Quantin, op. cit.

26. Ibid., p. 87; p. 85.

27. Ibid., p. 88.

28. Ibid., pp. 87-88. McGill also takes Aquinas to task: "According to Thomas Aquinas, also, man is only connected with the real through what is empirically actual." p. 88, note 187. He bases his judgement on Aquinas' belief that the mind is quite able to conceive of God's non-existence. (Summa contra Gentiles, I, 11). But so does Anselm: The term 'deus' must be replaced by description 'quo-maius-cogitari-nequit' in order to launch the argument.

29. Ibid., p. 89.

30. Ibid., pp. 89-93; 93-102. Aimé Forest, "L'argument de saint Anselme dans la philosophie reflexive" in Spicilegium Beccense, pp. 273-295. Also, D. Nicholl, "An Anselmian Soliloquy", in Downside Review, 1950, pp. 172-181, and J. Paliard, "Prière et dialectique", in Dieu Vivant 6 (1946), p. 57ff. Karl Barth, op. cit.

31. McGill, op. cit., p. 91.   32. Ibid., p. 92.

33. Idem.   34. Ibid., pp. 92-93.

35. Ibid., pp. 101-102. Epist. de Incar. Verbi, II, 20, 17-19.

36. Ibid., p. 102-104. The nineteenth century historians mentioned are: H. Bouchitte, La Rationalisme Chrétien (Paris, 1842); C. de Rémusat, S. Anselme de Cantorbéry (Paris, 1854); A Stockl, Geschichte der Philosophie des Mittelalters (Mainz, 1864), Vol. I; Van Weddingen, "Essai critique sur la phisophie de S. Anselme", in Mémoires Couronnes (Brussels, 1875), p. 103, note 225.

37. Ibid., p. 104; Proslogion, proemium, I, 93, 4-7.

38. Ibid., p. 104; Responsio, V, I, 135, 19ff; X, I, 138, 31.

39. Ibid., p. 105.   40. Idem.

41. Ibid., p. 109.   42. Idem.

43. Ibid., p. 110.

44. Id. McGill indicates that "the kind of reassessment that awaits Anselm has already been achieved in the case of Parmenides by Eugen Fink, in his Zur ontologischen Frühgeschichte von Raum - Zeit - Bewegung (The Hague, 1957), pp. 65-74." Ibid., p. 110, note 249.

45. William L. Rowe, "The Ontological Argument" in Reason and Responsibility, ed. J. Feinberg (Encino: Dickenson Publishing Co., 1974), p. 8.

46. Ibid., p. 10.

47. Ibid., p. 16.

48. Ibid., p. 17.

49. Richard Taylor, introduction to The Ontological Argument, ed. A. Plantiga (Garden City: Doubleday, 1965), p. xv.

50. Jerome Shaffer, "Existence, Predication and the Ontological Argument" in Mind, Vol. LXXI, N.S., No. 283, July 1962, reprinted in The Many-faced Argument, p. 226. By standard criticisms I refer to both that of illicit transition and existence is not a predicate.

51. Ibid., p. 228   52. Ibid., p. 242.

53. Ibid., pp. 242-243.   54. Ibid., p. 245.

55. Idem.

56. Gilbert Ryle, "Mr. Collingwood and the Ontological Argument", in _Mind_, Vol. XLIV, No. 174 (April, 1935), pp. 137-151; reprinted in _The Many-faced Argument_, pp. 246-260; "Back to the Ontological Argument", in _Mind_, Vol. XLVI, N.S. No. 181 (January, 1937), pp. 53-57; reprinted in _Ibid._, pp. 269-274.

57. "Mr. Collingwood....", p. 251.

58. _Ibid._, p. 252.

59. "Back to the Ontological Argument", pp. 273-274. See also G.E. Moore, "Is Existence a Predicate," in _Proceedings of the Aristotelian Society_, Vol. XV, 1936.

60. William P. Alston, "The Ontological Argument Revisited", in _The Philosophical Review_, Vol. XLIX (1960), reprinted in _The Ontological Argument_, p. 86.

61. _Ibid._, p. 93. The 'standard argument' is given by Alston as follows: before we can attach a predicate to anything we must presuppose that it exists. If we were not making that assumption, we could not even raise the question whether a given predicate attaches to it. Hence, we can predicate or refuse to predicate anything of a perfect being only if we purport to have already settled that there is a perfect being. p. 89-90.

62. _Ibid._, p. 94.   63. _Ibid._, p. 98.

64. _Ibid._, p. 101.   65. _Ibid._, pp. 102-103.

66. _Ibid._, pp. 107-108. "King Arthur really existed. Arthur exists in legend and in reality, that is, we want to treat both modes of existence on a par, as having the same connection to Arthur. But on a subject-predicate interpretation this would not be the case. Real existence would be predicated of the legendary figure, but legendary existence would not be predicated of the real figure." (p. 108).

67. _Ibid._, p. 110.   68. _Ibid._, p. 98.

69. _Ibid._, p. 104.

70. Norman Malcolm, "Anselm's Ontological Arguments" in the _Philosophical Review_, Vol. LXIX (1960), reprinted in _The Ontological Argument_, pp. 138-159.

71. _Ibid._, p. 140.   72. _Idem._

73. _Ibid._, p. 141.   74. _Ibid._, p. 142.

75. Ibid., p. 145.

76. "Human beings formed the concept of 'an infinite being' because of overwhelming guilt, greater than which cannot be conceived." Ibid., p. 158.

77. Ibid., p. 159   78. Idem.

79. Paul Henle, "Uses of the Ontological Argument", in The Philosophical Review, Vol. LXX (1961), reprinted in The Ontological Argument, pp. 172-180; esp. p. 172.

80. Ibid., pp. 172-173.

81. "Necessary existence is a property of God in the same sense that necessary omnipotence and necessary omniscience are his properties." Malcolm, op. cit., p. 147.

82. Henle, op. cit., p. 175.   83. Ibid., p. 178.

84. Ibid., pp. 179-180.   85. Ibid., p. 179.

86. Jasper Hopkins, A Companion to the Study of St. Anselm (Minneapolis: University of Minnesota Press, 1972).

87. Appendix I. Anselm's Philosophical Fragments, op. cit., pp. 215-242. Refer to F.S. Schmitt, Ein neues unvollendetes werk des hl. Anselm von Canterbury (Beiträge zur Geschichte der Philosophie und Theologie der Mittelalters, 33/3), Münster, 1936.

88. Refer especially to Ibid., p. 135ff. and p. 85ff.

89, Ibid., pp. 67-89. However, one may profit greatly from a reading of his interesting 'Anselm's Debate with Gaunilo' in Analecta Anselmiana, V.

90. Ibid., p. 85.   91. Ibid., p. 83.

92. Ibid., p. 77; 89.

93. A study which is not included in this outline because it requires substantive treatment is Jules Vuillemin, Le Dieu d'Anselme et Les Aparences de la Raison (Paris: Aubier Montaigne, 1971).

CONCLUSION

This introductory study of the _Proslogion_ should end with a backwards glance at the Fool, the personification of the enigmatic character of the treatise. He bows out in the fourth chapter, illustrating the moment intellige ut credas which precedes the crede ut intelligas. Although understanding does not generate faith, it remains, as has been indicated, its necessary precondition as without prior understanding faith is impossible. This understanding prior to faith provides the ground for its very possibility. The understanding consequent on faith guides the believer towards his ultimate goal - the vision of God. It is a therapeutic activity which prepares him for entry into a domain which transcends his noetic possibilities.

The Fool, insofar as he is a Fool, is limited to the first type of understanding. Only fiath, uniting justice with truth, can enable him to arrive at that unique understanding which is generated by faith. Nonetheless, the development of the _Proslogion_ argument, as a piece of rational work, is open to view. He is able to subject it to the scrutiny of rigorous thought. It may even help to activate his piritual possibilities, though several obstacles are encountered on the way.

The Fool's denial of God's existence is only possible on the level of vox and not on the level of res: if He is to think of God at all, the Fool must think of God as existing. Furthermore, this denial betrays both spiritual and intellectual weakness, as it violates the principal of non-contradiction, intelligibility, and the very structure of possibility. The Fool may have succumbed to Anselm's argument but on this point the text is silent. On the other hand, he may well have composed his own Pro Insipiente. As has been indicated, outside of the ambit of faith, knowledge by itself is not therapeutic. It is merely a 'seed' that can be activated by God. Divine intervention is required in both the spiritual and intellectual domains. Without it, the Fool would never be liberated from his foolishness. It is conceivable that the Fool be convinced by the argument and yet remain a Fool, assent intellectually to the existence of a Necessary Being but still be far from the God of faith.

It has been stressed that reason, in Anselm's opinion, is primarilly displayed in the moral order, by distinguishing good from evil. Through loving and appropriating the good while

condemning and rejecting evil, the rational soul is transformed
into a loving soul, directed to the enjoyment of God. Knowledge
restricted to the cognitive order, would be a truncated thing at
best, contradicting the very purpose of creation. Faith is required so that reason be faithful to itself, so that full rationality be restored to it. In a sense, the Proslogion is an account of the progressive metamorphosis of reason in the soul's
pilgrimage to God.

Anselm and the Fool meet at the very beginning of this journey on the common ground of reason and a shared humanity. Anselm
not only refutes the Fool's claim that God does not exist but in
so doing manifests the efficacy of reason not illumined by faith
and uncovers the inner exigencies by which reason is propelled
towards its transcendent fulfillment. This is why the Fool's
early exit from the Proslogion can best be understood as
Anselm's tribute to the mystery of God's action on man.

It is from the Fool's vantage point that the distortions
and misrepresentations of the argument can be most profitably
considered. The rigorous, incisive, dialectic of Proslogion II-
IV,directed against the negation of God's existence, makes the
mystical, 'knight of faith' hypothesis untenable. The restrained
effusion of the chapters following the Fool's exit discourages any
hyper-rationalist interpretation. Anselm was decidedly not
balancing faith and reason by the sheer force of his personality.
He was viewing both as complementary moments of a single process,
a complementarity which can be seen by contrasting the Fool with
the believer, who both seeks to understand what he believes and
to raise his mind to the contemplation of God.

Undoubtedly, man's relation to God is to a great extent a
thought relation simply because God is revealed to a greater
extent in the human soul (the trinitarian image) than in the
exterior world. The movement from reason, the privileged point
of departure, to God is a sort of prayer. Rigorous thought and
prayer are not separate activities but part of this one movement
towards the possession and fruition of God. Anselm insists that
to think rigorously about God under the aegis of faith entails
the ascent to God. Thought with regard to God which is not a
kind of prayer is not true thought.

The description of God as 'something-than-which-nothing-
greater-can-be-thought' provides Anselm and the Fool with a
starting point for the argument. It moves from general to necessary existence, finally arriving at an existence which transcends thought. But faith has not disappeared from the scene as
it exercises a negative control by which reason is kept true to
itself, nisi credidero, non inteligam. Anselm's rationalism
consists in viewing faith as the necessary corrective to arrive

at that full rationality which was destroyed by the Fall. The
rather ambiguous term gnosis was used to describe the unique
nature of the Proslogion, both demonstration and meditation.

Anselm continued the tradition of classic theoria but displaced it from the theoretical to the practical order, from speculation to the order of love. The noéséos noésis cannot really
be identified with the sapientia quae omnia condidit ex nihilo.
He approaches Christian contemplatio though in the Proslogion
Anselm stops short of the properly mystical. He insists that a
real encounter with God cannot be limited to demonstration - not
even the proof that God exists - but must include experience, an
experience which adumbrates the plenitude of joy of the beatific
vision. There is a continuity between the present and the future
life: the more one advances in understanding the closer he approaches vision. Knowledge, love, and joy (in hope), commence
in this life to be made complete in the next.

Anselm made the important discovery that human thought is
able to construct a description of God, 'something-than-which-
nothing-greater-can-be-thought' which, when unpacked dialectically
by means of the principal of non-contradiction, leads to the affirmation of the existence of a Necessary Being. Human thought
is rooted in God and to think God, even under the rubric of this
description, is a reaching out towards Him, a transition from
the relative non-being of contingent things to the necessary
being of God. The verbal formulation of the God-description acts
as the bridge which connects the vox to the res signified. God's
necessity is viewed as displaying itself within the noetic order.

A domain is discovered in which the dichotomy between the
conceptual and the real is transcended: to think this being is to
think it as existing necessarily. As it is thought to exist necessarily it must be at least a possible being. But it cannot
be limited to the domain of possibility because it has none of
the limitations of contingent beings,either possible or real.
The transition which takes place is not simply from existence in
intellectu to existence in re, but, if traced out, from conceptual existence to necessary existence (in the mind) to necessary
existence, outside of the mind. Anselm suggests that thinking
itself possesses a superabundance which transcends its human,
contingent mode, reflected in the God-description. A dynamism is
discovered within human thinking which marches from contingent to
necessary existence. Adumbrating the later theory of the analogy
of being, he indicates that 'being' applies to God and to creatures in different ways.

Gaunilo was correct in suggesting that the Proslogion argument could be rejected if the God-description were meaningless.
Alert to the strength of this objection, Anselm took extraordinary

care to prove that the description is understood. The intelligibility of the description is the cornerstone of the argument as well as its point of departure. If it were meaningless, it would not be 'in the understanding' (possess conceptual existence) and the argument would have to be aborted. But the Fool's own denial of God's existence implies at least some understanding of what is denied. Moreover, the description is not open to the objections that the term 'God' is subject to.

The task undertaken in the present study is not precisely a modest one: to reinterpret the Proslogion within the framework of Anselm's culture and thought and to provide a basis for the study of the later transformations of the argument. Textual interpretation was followed by analyses of Anselm's conception of reason, it's relation to faith, and necessary reasons. The major medieval, contemporary, and modern objections, together with restatements of the argument, were also taken into account. The first part of the study, the 'archeological', rests on decidedly firmer ground than the second which is somewhat more speculative. The clearing away of debris is a far easier task than the work of construction.

The main question has yet to be answered. Is the Proslogion argument demonstrative? Has Anselm proved the existence of God? Has he proved anything at all? The Proslogion as gnosis can only be verified in the afterlife as the privileged experience of joy is found only through hope in the present life. Does the argument as a work of reason also wait upon eternity? The verdict would then be superfluous. The most that can be said is that the argument is demonstrative if the complex web of Anselm's presuppositions is accepted. Perhaps this is too much to ask. In any event, the study of the philosophical and theological ground of the Proslogion should be continued and extended. In this way perhaps the task will become progressively less cumbersome.

Nonetheless, the argument does enjoy a certain consistency which is reflected on the superficial level by its status as a classic as well as by the lack of a definitive refutation. To attack it seems to mobilize its strength and weigh reason in its favor. The argument is decidedly queer. Even if Anselm were successful in proving the existence of a necessary being, its later transformation into the God of Christianity, the God of faith, would be a task which surpasses the rational order. At this point, it may be wise to repeat with Anselm, "non sunt verba tantum audienda sed est res terrifice metuenda".

SELECTED BIBLIOGRAPHY

I. PROSLOGION TEXT

A. LATIN

St. Anselm Opera Omnia, edited by Dom Francis de Sales Schmitt,
6 volumes (Edinburgh: Thomas Nelson, 1945-1951). Vol. I,
101-104; 125-139. Also J. P. Migne, Patrologia Latina, 158
(1863), 227-229; 241-260.

B. ENGLISH TRANSLATION

St. Anselm Proslogion: Monologion: an Appendix in Behalf of the
Fool by Gaunilo; and Cur Deus Homo? Translated by Sidney
N. Deane (La Salle, Ill.: Open Court Publishing House,
1903; Rev. ed., St. Anselm: Basic Writings, 1962).

A Scholastic Miscellany: Anselm to Ockham, edited and translated
by E.R. Fairweather (London: S.C.M. Press, and Philadelphia:
Westminster Press, 1956). This contains the Proslogion and
an extract from Anselm's reply to Gaunilo.

St. Anselm's "Proslogion" with "A Reply on Behalf of the Fool"
by Gaunilo and "The Author's Reply to Gaunilo," translated
with an introduction and philosophical commentary by M.J.
Charlesworth (Oxford: The Claredon Press, 1965).

The Ontological Argument from St. Anselm to Contemporary Philoso-
phers, edited by A. Plantinga, with an introduction by
Richard Taylor (Garden City, N.Y.: Doubleday, 1965). This
contains the first four chapters of the Proslogion, and both
Gaunilo's In Behalf of the Fool and St. Anselm's Reply.
(Deane Translation).

C. FRENCH TRANSLATION

Oeuvres Philosophiques de Saint Anselme, translated by P. Rousseau
(Paris: Aubier, 1945); Proslogion, Pro Insipiente, and
Responsio, pp. 175-221.

Koyré, A. Saint Anselme de Cantorbery: Fides Quaerens Intellectum
(Paris: Vrin, 1964).

D. SPANISH TRANSLATION

Obras Completas de San Anselmo (Latin-Spanish), translated by J.
Alameda, O.S.B. (Madrid: B.A.C., 1952-1953), II Vols.;
Proslogion, Pro Insipiente, Responsio, Vol. I, pp. 358-437.

E. GERMAN TRANSLATION

Schmitt, Franciscus Salesius. Anselm von Canterbury, Proslogion.
Lateinisch-deutsche Ausgabe von ...., (Stuttgart-Bad
Cannstatt, 1962).

F. ITALIAN TRANSLATION

Sandri, Giuseppe. Anselm d'Aosta, Il Proslogion, Le Orazioni e
Le Meditazione. Introduzione e testo Latino di F.S. Schmitt.
(Padova, 1959).

II. ANSELMIANA: COLLECTIONS

Analecta Anselmiana: Untersuchungen über Person und Werk Anselms
von Canterbury, edited by K. Flasch, B. Geyer, R. W.
Southern (Frankfurt/Main: Minerva GMBH), Vol. I (1970),
Voo. II (1971), Vol. III (1972), Vol. IV (1974), Vol. V
(1976).

Revue de philosophie, 15 (1909). The entire issue is dedicated
to Anselm's sources and thought.

Sola Ratione, Anselm-Studien für Pater Dr. h.c. Franciscus
Salesius Schmitt, O.S.B., zum 75 Gebartstag. Edited by H.K.
Kohlenberger (Stuttgart: F. Fromman Verlag, 1970).

Spicilegium Beccense, edited by P. Grammont and the monks of
Abbaye Notre-Dame du Bec (Paris: Vrin, 1959).

The Many-faced Argument, edited by J. Hick and A.C. McGill (New
York: The Macmillan Company, 1967).

III. THE PROSLOGION ARGUMENT IN THE
CONTEXT OF MEDIEVAL THOUGHT

Cappuyns, Maïeul. "L'argument de saint Anselme" in Recherches de Theólogie ancienne et médiévale 6 (1934), 313-330.

Dal Pra, Mario. "Il problema del fondamento del significato nella controversia Tra Anselmo e Gaunilo" in Rivista critica di storia della filosofia, 9 (1954), 132-155.

Forest, A., von Steenberghen, F. and de Gandillac, M. Le Movement doctrinale du XIe au XIVe siècle (Paris: Bloud et Gay, 1956), pp. 31-68.

Gilson, É. History of Christian Philosophy in the Middle Ages (New York: Random House, 1955), p. 128ff.

_____. The Spirit of Medieval Philosophy, trans. by A.C. Downes (New York: Charles Scribner's Sons, 1936), Chapter 3.

_____. "Sens et nature de l'argument de Saint Anselme", in Archives d'histoire doctrinale et littéraire du moyen age, 9 (1934), 5-51.

Grabmann, M. Geschichte der scholastischen metode (Freiburg im Breisgau: Herder, 1909), I, Part 5.

Leclercq, Jean. L'Amour des lettres et le désir de Dieu, trans. C. Misrahi, The Love of Learning and the Desire for God (New York: Mentor Omega, 1961), pp. 215ff to 271ff.

Leclercq, J., Vandenbroucke, F., et Bouyer, L. La Spiritualité du Moyen Age (Paris: Aubier, 1961), trans. by the Benedictines of Holme Eden Abbey, The Spirituality of the Middle Ages (London: Barns and Oates, 1968, pp. 162-167.

Pieper, Josef. Scholastik, trans. R. Cercos, Filosofía Medieval y Mundo Moderno (Madrid: Ediciones Rialp, 1973), pp. 67-93.

Stolz, Anselm. "Das Proslogion des hl. Anselm" in Revue Benedictine, 47 (1935), 331-347.

Vanni-Rovighi, Sofia. S. Anselmo e la filosofia del Secolo XI (Milano: Fratelli Boca, 1949), esp. p. 81ff.

_____. "Questo mirabili secolo XII", in <u>Studium</u> 54, 1958).

Vignaux, Paul. "La méthode de Saint Anselme dans le Monologion et le Proslogion", in <u>Aquinas</u> 8 (1965), 110-129.

IV. THE PROSLOGION ARGUMENT IN THE
CONTEXT OF ANSELM'S THOUGHT

Barth, Karl. <u>Fides quaerens intellectum</u>: <u>Anselms Beweis der Existence Gottes im Zusammenhang sienes theologischen Programms</u> (1st ed., Munich; Chr. Kaiser Verlag, 1931), trans. S.C.M. Press, 1960), Richmond: John Knox Press, 1960, and Cleveland: Meridian Books, 1962).

Kohlenberger, Helmut. <u>Similitudo und Ratio</u>: <u>Überlegungen zur Methode bei Anselm von Canterbury</u> (Bonn: Bouvier Verlag Herbert Grundmann, 1972).

Kolping, Adolf. <u>Anselms Proslogion - Beweis der Existenz Gottes im Zussamenhang seines spekulativen Programms</u>: <u>Fides Quaerens Intellectum</u> (Bonn: Hanstein, 1939).

Koyré, A. <u>L'Idée de Dieu dans la philosophie de S. Anselme</u> (Paris: J. Vrin, 1923).

Marias, Julian. <u>San Anselmo y el Insensato</u> (Madrid: Revista de Occidente, 1954).

Moreau, Joseph. <u>Pour ou contre l'insensé? Essai sur la preuve Anselmienne</u> (Paris: Vrin, 1967).

Rist, John M. "Notes on Anselm's Aims in the Proslogion" in <u>Vivarium</u> 11, 109-118) N 73.

Rousseau, Pierre, "Note sur la connaissance de Dieu selon saint Anselme", in <u>De La Connaissance de Dieu</u> (Paris: Recherches de philosophie, 1958), 177-185.

Schmitt, F.S. "Der ontologische Gottesbeweis Anselms" in <u>Theologische Revue</u>, 32 (1933), 217-233.

Schmitt, Franciscus Salesius. "Anselm von Canterbury" in <u>Lexicon fur Theologie und Kirche</u> (Freiburg Br., z. Aufl., 1957), 592-594.

Vuillemin, Jules. <u>Le Dieu D'Anselme et Les Aparences de la Raison</u> (Paris: Aubier Montaigne, 1971).

V. SPECIAL STUDIES OF ANSELM'S ARGUMENT

Adlhoch, B. "Der Gottesbeweis des hl. Anselm", in Philosophische Jahrbuch der Görres-Gesellschaft, 8 (1895), 52-69, 372-389; 9 (1896), 280-297; 10 (1897), 261-274, 394-416; 16 (1903), 163-170, 300-309; 21 (1908), 288-292.

Allshouse, Merle. An Evaluation of Anselm's Ontological Argument (unpublished dissertation) (Ann Arbor, No. 66-48ff; University Microfilms).

Barnes, Jonathan. The Ontological Argument (London: Macmillan Press, 1972).

Berg, Jan. "An Examination of the Ontological Proof", in Theoria, 27 (1961) 99-106.

Caird, Edward. "Anselm's Argument for the Being of God", in the Journal of Theological Studies, I (1899), 23-39.

Dondeyne, A. "De argumento S. Anselmi", in Collationes Brugenses, 30 (1930), 126-131.

Hartshorne, Charles. The Logic of Perfection and Other Essays in Neoclassical Metaphysics (La Salle: The Open Court Publishing Co., 1962).

_____. Anselm's Discovery: A Re-examination of the Ontological Proof for the Existence of God (La Salle: Open Court, 1962).

Henry, D. P. "The Proslogion Proofs", in Philosophical Quarterly, 5 (1955), 147-151.

LaCroix, Richard R. Proslogion II and III: A Third Interpretation of Anselm's Argument (Leiden, Brill, 1972).

Malcolm, Norman. "Anselm's Ontological ARguments", in the Philosophical Review, Vol. LXIX (1960). Philosophical Review, 70 (1961), 56-111; discussion by: Allen, R.E. "Ontological Argument", 56-66; Abelson, R. "Not Necessarily", 67-84; Penelhum, T. "On the Second Ontological Argument", 85-92; Plantinga, A. "Valid Ontological Argument", 93-101.

Moreau, Joseph. Pour ou contre l'insensé? Essai sur la preuve Anselmienne (Paris: Vrin, 1967).

Nicholl, D. "An Anselmian Soliloquy"in <u>Downside Review</u>, 1950, 172-181.

Paliard, J. "Priere et dialectique", in <u>Dieu Vivant</u>, 6 (1946), p. 57ff.

Rowe, William L. "The ontological Argument", in <u>Reason and Responsibility</u>, ed. J. Feinberg (Encino: Dickenson Publishing Co., 1974), pp. 8-17.

Smart, Hugh R. "Anselm's Ontological Argument: Rationalistic or Apologetic?", in <u>Review of Metaphysics</u>, 3 (1949), 161-166.

Stolz, A. "Zur Theologie Anselms in <u>Proslogion</u>", in <u>Catholica</u> 2 (1933), 1-24. Translated by A.C. McGill, <u>The Many-faced Argument</u>, pp. 183-206.

_____. "Das <u>Proslogion</u> des hl. Anselm", in <u>Revue Benedictine</u>, 47 (1935), 331-347.

Wolz, H.G. "Empirical Basis of Anselm's Arguments" in <u>Philosophical Review</u>, 60 (1951), 341-361.

VI. OTHER STUDIES RELEVANT TO THE PROSLOGION ARGUMENT

Bayert, J. "The Concept of Mystery according to St. Anselm of Canterbury" in <u>Recherches de Théologie ancienne et mediévale</u>, 9 (1937), 125-166.

Henry D.P. <u>The De Grammatico of St. Anselm</u> (Notre Dame: University of Notre Dame Press, 1964).

_____. <u>The Logic of St. Anselm</u> (Oxford: Claredon Press, 1967).

Jacquin, A. M. "Les rationes necessariae de Saint Anselme", in <u>Melanges Mandonnet</u> (Paris: Vrin, 1930) II, pp. 67-78.

Koch, Josef. "Augustinischer und dionysischer Neuplatonismus und Mittelalter" in <u>Kant-Studien</u>, 48 (1956/57), pp. 117-133.

Losacco, M. "La dialettica in Anselmo d'Aosta", in <u>Sophia</u> 1 (1933), 188-193.

McIntyre, John. <u>St. Anselm and His Critics</u>. (Edinburgh: Oliver and Boyd, 1954).

Ottaviano, C. "Les rationes necessariae de St. Anselme", in
    Sophia, I (1933), 92-97.

Phelan, P. The Wisdom of St. Anselm (Latrobe, Pa.: Archabbey
    Press, 1960).

Pouchet, Robert. La Rectitude chez Saint Anselme (Paris: Etudes
    Augustiniennes, 1964).

Roques, Rene. "La methode de s. Anselme dans le Cur Deus Homo",
    in Aquinas 5 (1962), 3-57.

_____. Anselme de Canterbery: Porquoi Dieu s'est fait homme.
    Texte Latin, introduction, bibliographie, traduction et
    notes. Serie des textes monastiques d'Occident 11 (Paris:
    Sources chretiennes 91, 1963).

Schmitt, Franciscus Salesius. "Zur Chronologie der Werke des hl.
    Anselm von Canterbury", Revue benedictine 43 (1932), 322-
    350.

Southern, R.W. St. Anselm and his Biographer (Cambridge: C.U.P.
    1963).

Vignaux, Paul. "Structure et sens du Monologion", in Revue des
    sciences philosophiques et théologiques, 31 (1947), 192-
    212.

VII. THE ONTOLOGICAL ARGUMENT IN THE
CONTEXT OF MODERN THOUGHT

Belaval, Yvon. Leibniz Critique de Descartes (Paris: Gallimard,
    1960), pp. 532-536.

The Philosophical Works of Descartes, trans. Haldon & Ross
    (London: Cambridge University Press, 1967), II Vols.
    Meditations on first Philosophy, Vol. I, pp. 133-199,
    Objections, Vol. II, pp. 1-344.

Gouhier, H. "La Preuve ontologique de Descartes" in Revue Inter-
    nationale de philosophie, 8 (1954), 295-303.

Gueroult, M. Nouvelles Réflexions sur la Preuve Ontologique de
    Descartes (Paris: J. Vrin, 1955).

Hegel, G.W.F. Vorlesungen über die Philosophie der Religion,
    trans. Spiers & Sanderson, Lectures in the Philosophy of
    Religion (New York: The Humanities Press, 1962), Vol. III.

_____. Vorlesungen über die Geschichte der Philosophie, trans. Haldane & Simposn, Lectures on the History of Philosophy (New York: The Humanities Press, 1965).

Kant, I. Kritik der Reinen Vernunft, trans. by N. Kemp-Smith Immanuel Kant's Critique of Pure Reason (New York: St. Martin's Press, 1961), A591, B619ff.

Koyré, A. Essai sur L'Idee de Dieu et les preuves de son existence chez Descartes (Paris: Vrin, 1922).

Lauer, Quentin. "Hegel on Proofs for God's Existence" in Kant-Studien (Köln: Kölner Universitats-Verlag, 1964), pp. 443-465.

Leibniz, G. W. Nouveaux Essais, trans. with notes by A. G. Langley, New Essays (La Salle: Open Court, 1949), Book IV, Chapter X.

VIII. THE ONTOLOGICAL ARGUMENT IN RECENT PHILOSOPHICAL LITERATURE

Alston, William P. "The Ontological Argument Revisited", in the Philosophical Review, Vol. XLIX (1960).

Balz, A. G. "Concerning the Ontological Argument", in Review of Metaphysics, 7 (1935), 207-224.

Collingwood, R. G. An Essay on Philosophical Method (Oxford: Clarendon Press, 1933).

Dominquez-Berrueta, Juan. "El Argumento Ontologico", in Verdad y Vida, I (1943), 370-376.

Findlay, J. N. "Can God's Existence be Disproved?", in Mind, 57 (1948), 176-183.

Harris, E. E. Revelation Through Reason (New Haven: Yale University Press, 1958), 53-63; 88-94.

_____. "Mr. Collingwood and the Ontological Argument", in Mind, 44 (1935), 137-151.

Henle, Paul. "Uses of the Ontological Argument", in The Philosophical Review, Vol. XLIX (1960).

Hick, John. "God as Necessary Being", in The Journal of Philosophy, Vol. 57 (1960), pp. 725-734.

_____. "Ontological Argument for the Existence of God", in *The Encyclopedia of Philosophy* 5 (1967), 538ff.

Ryle, Gilbert. "Mr. Collingwood and the Ontological Argument", in *Mind*, Vol. XLIV, No. 174 (April, 1935), 137-151.

_____. "Back to the Ontological Argument" in *Mind*, Vol. XLVI, N.S. No. 181 (January,1937), pp. 53-57.

Shaffer, Jerome. "Existence, Predication and the Ontological Argument", in *Mind*, Vol. LXXI, N.S. No. 283, (July, 1962).

Taylor, Richard. "Introduction", *The Ontological Argument* (Garden City: Doubleday, 1965), VII-XVIII.

Tillich, Paul. "The Two Types of Philosophy of Religion", in *Theology of Culture* (New York: O.U.P., 1959).

Wolz, H. G. "The Empirical Basis of Anselm's Arguments", in *Philosophical Review*, 60 (1951), 341-361.